I highly recommend this book to anyone wanting to experience greater freedom and intimacy with the Lord. Linda Godsey is an anointed minister and author. She has real-life experience as a pastor who has helped many people. This isn't just a book that will change your life—it can also change your family for generations.

—Jimmy Evans
Founder and CEO
Marriage Today

Understanding the impact of our "origins" can create a pathway for true freedom. Linda Godsey is a seasoned pastor whose main focus of ministry has been centered on liberating believers from the lies of the enemy. I wholeheartedly recommend this book as a pathway for personal freedom and as a toolbox to those in this area of ministry. *Origins* will help you change the course of your family legacy for generations to come.

—Bobby Bogard
Associate Senior Pastor
Gateway Church

Linda Godsey has a rare quality of being able to get to the heart of a matter. Sitting in her presence for a few moments somehow unlocks the mysteries of the human heart and creates an environment of safety, love, and truth, and before you know it, clarity, freedom, and hope begin to pour through her into the lives of others. She's anointed to discern spiritual matters while leading others to practical, clear, breakthrough revelation. I highly recommend this book—and this woman—to anyone who wants to experience a greater understanding of the spiritual world and how we can walk in more love, power, and freedom.

Origins isn't just a how-to book; this is a playbook that will help you change your legacy.

—Jan Greenwood
Pastor, Pink, Gateway Women
Author, *Women at War*

It is with deep gratitude and appreciation to my dear friend Linda Godsey that I recommend this book to anyone who is seeking to find the freedom the Lord Jesus died to give humanity. These truths, shared out of Linda's years of ministry, were used by the Lord in my own life to release the bondage in my generational line. *Origins* will bless you with testimonies of others who have found new levels of freedom from generational iniquity. So don't hesitate. Read on and let the Lord bring liberation to you and your future generations.

—Tommy Briggs, Sr.
Associate Pastor, Freedom Ministries
Gateway Church

This work has the fingerprints and heart of our Savior all over it! Having dealt with large numbers of believers and unbelievers alike for many years, I have found one thing to be true: our familial past heavily affects our present freedom. Linda is one of the most anointed, knowledge-able, and effective ministers on this subject anywhere, and the church has needed this resource for years. *Origins* will lead in transforming churches, communities, and, most of all, our own precious families for generations to come.

—Byron Copeland
Executive Campus Pastor
Gateway Church North Richland Hills

ORIGINS.

LINDA GODSEY

GATEWAY
CREATE
PUBLISHING

Most CHARISMA HOUSE BOOK GROUP products are available at special quantity discounts for bulk purchase for sales promotions, premiums, fund-raising, and educational needs. For details, write Charisma House Book Group, 600 Rinehart Road, Lake Mary, Florida 32746, or telephone (407) 333-0600.

ORIGINS by Linda Godsey
Published by Gateway Create Publishing
Gateway Create Publishing
700 Blessed Way
Southlake, TX 76092
www.gatewaycreate.com

Unless otherwise noted, all Scripture quotations are taken from The Holy Bible, New International Version®, NIV®. Copyright © 1973, 1978, 1984, 2011 by Biblica, Inc.™ Used by permission of Zondervan. All rights reserved worldwide. www .zondervan.com. The "NIV" and "New International Version" are trademarks registered in the United States Patent and Trademark Office by Biblica, Inc.™

Scripture quotations marked AMP are from the Amplified Bible. Copyright © 1954, 1958, 1962, 1964, 1965, 1987 by The Lockman Foundation. Used by permission.

Scripture quotations marked ASV are from the American Standard Bible.

Scripture quotations marked ESV are from the Holy Bible, English Standard Version. Copyright © 2001 by Crossway

Cover design by Lisa Rae McClure
Design Director: Justin Evans

Visit the author's website at www.lindagodsey.com.

International Standard Book Number: 978-1-62998-590-9
E-book ISBN: 978-1-62998-700-2

While the author has made every effort to provide accurate
Internet addresses at the time of publication, neither the
publisher nor the author assumes any responsibility for errors
or for changes that occur after publication.

First edition

16 17 18 19 20 — 987654321
Printed in the United States of America

Gateway Create gratefully acknowledges the partnership of
Charisma House in distributing this book.

Dedicated to my six amazing grandchildren: Corey, Kyle, Colson, Quinn, London, and Owen. You have brought me so much joy. I had the awesome privilege of being present at each one of your births and to remain radically involved in your lives. Each of you are uniquely wired, gifted, talented, and precious to me. I'm so proud of you! You inspire me to pursue my own freedom and leave a godly legacy.

A good person leaves an inheritance
for their children's children.
—Proverbs 13:22, NIV

CONTENTS

Chapter 1

YOUR ORIGINS MATTER

C AN YOU THINK of a trait in your family of origin that you dislike? Or, on the flip side, are there characteristics you really appreciate about your family? Chances are, you can identify both good and bad qualities in your family line. Most families have traits to be admired and desired, along with some we would like to sweep under the rug, never to be remembered again.

A woman came to meet with me some time ago. As she sat down, I asked her the usual question: "What brings you here today?" She replied, "Have you ever seen the television series *Everybody Loves Raymond*? Well, that is my family—total dysfunction!" We had a good laugh; but as she told me her story, I realized that she was telling the truth.

The majority of us have inherited both good and bad family characteristics. Occasionally someone will say to me, "I can't think of a single good trait in my family." Still others insist, "My family was a *Leave It to Beaver* family, and I can't think of anything I would want to change." Most of the time neither extreme is true. No family is perfect, and very few are deficient in every single area.

Bible teacher Beth Moore, in her book *Breaking Free*, wrote: "Between every unfaithful generation and faithful generation is one person determined to change."[1] Whether or not we break unhealthy generational iniquity and ungodly patterns is a matter of the heart. That's where the battle is being waged—over the heart! No matter who we are or how we grew up, the question we all must answer is: Whom will we serve?

A SPIRITUAL EYE-OPENER

I remember a special insight God gave me one morning many years ago. My husband had left for work earlier than usual, so I had the house all to myself when I returned from taking the children to school. Sitting down at the dining room table, my Bible in hand, I began reading and felt drawn to Isaiah 58:12:

> Those from among you shall rebuild the old waste places; you shall raise up the foundations of many generations.
>
> —MEV

Although Bible scholars say this passage is about the restoration and redevelopment of Jerusalem, I knew the Lord was personalizing it for me. That promise to Israel was predicated upon their returning to the true worship that comes from a pure heart. Since their works didn't match the claims of their faith, God wanted to change their hearts.

As I meditated on the passage, I saw in my mind's eye (some would call it a vision) a country setting with an old, run-down house that sat on a large parcel of land. I saw a bulldozer lift the house from its pier-and-beam foundation. When it was raised, I could see all sorts of bugs, mold, mildew, and other gross things you would see underneath an old house that has been in place for years. That house clearly needed to be renovated, and I realized this picture, or vision, represented the spiritual restoration that needed to happen in my life.

At that time the subject of generational iniquity was new to me. But I recognized that the Isaiah passage, along with the picture I had seen of the old house being lifted from its foundation, was the Lord's way of showing me that I was under the influence of the choices some of my ancestors had made. In some cases I had been a willing participant in making some of the same decisions they had made, both consciously and unconsciously.

I knew God wanted to do some spiritual cleanup in me. For the first time in my life I began to connect the dots between my current struggles and the deeper root systems that had been established before I was in my mother's womb.

As I began to seek the Lord concerning this need for spiritual renovation, I felt Him speak four clear statements to my heart:

1. "I want to rebuild the foundations of your life."

2. "I desire to change your heart and create new heart attitudes."

3. "I long to release heart worship in you."

4. "I want to establish new thinking or godly belief systems." (In other words, learn to think like God thinks.)

When he was speaking at our church many years ago, I heard John Sandford, author of *Healing the Wounded Spirit*,[2] say, "When we have dealt with our own personal sin and trouble still persists, we may be dealing with generational sin and iniquity." Clearly this is not an excuse for bad behavior and poor choices, but generational sin is often responsible for creating weakness and temptation toward certain behavior. It is a delusion to believe we can sin without it affecting others. It always does!

I once knew a man who confided to a pastor/counselor that he never watched pornography in front of his young son. He said, "I wait until he has gone to bed." He obviously didn't understand that in addition to having physical bodies, we are spiritual beings who transmit spiritual genetics. The choices we make affect our children and future generations.

Thankfully we have the awesome privilege and powerful opportunity to begin a new heritage and leave a godly legacy for our children and grandchildren. That spiritual and moral legacy will not only bless them, but it will also glorify God as well.

I firmly believe it is crucial for Christians to understand how the choices of our ancestors still affect us today. Unfortunately this seems to be one of the most neglected subjects in the church. Recently our church held a freedom event where I taught on generational iniquity. Afterward a few of our pastors took some of the visiting ministers to dinner. During their time together several of them expressed how deeply touched and transformed they had been by the teaching on generational iniquity and bloodline curses. They had never been exposed to the subject, and they were amazed at the impact it had on them. It is especially exciting to see pastors receive God's wisdom in this area because then they are better equipped to minister these life-changing truths to the people in their churches.

Ax Laid to the Root

It is helpful to discover the tendencies toward particular sins and patterns of negative behavior that existed in our families long before we were born. Discovering those potential snares better prepares us to make right choices and come into alignment with the ultimate authority: the Word of God. When we agree with what God says, we can recognize ungodly mind-sets and behavior patterns and allow the power of the Holy Spirit to break those tendencies. Then we will experience freedom from the consequences of sin that may have been operating for generations.

A few years ago one of our pastors at Gateway Church in Southlake, Texas, was teaching a Wednesday night topical freedom class. In his message he mentioned that if a person had experienced repeated accidents, it could be the result of a generational curse. He had barely spoken those words when a woman in the class began to cry.

The pastor asked me to take the woman to the prayer room and minister to her while he continued his teaching. In the prayer room the woman began to tell me her story. She had been in a number of accidents over the past few years. If that were not enough, she was also facing a financial crisis and would be going to court within the next few days. Additionally she told me a young family member had recently been diagnosed with a brain tumor, and she and her family were praying for him to be healed. (I later discovered that my daughter, an RN at the hospital where the young boy had surgery, took care of him in Pediatric ICU afterward. What a small world! God's fingerprints were all over the scheduling of that surgery.)

In situations like this I'm glad I know the Wonderful Counselor and Great Physician—Jesus! The Holy Spirit led me to ask her to quiet her heart and listen for His voice. I then asked the Holy Spirit, "Is there any kind of curse over this family that You want to reveal tonight? Is there any transgression that has been committed that she needs to repent of and renounce? Has anything recent or from the past opened a door for the enemy to harass her and her family?"

Before I could continue, she lifted her head and said, "Oh my. I would have never thought of that!" She explained to me that her family name and heritage were German. Recently, she confided, her brothers had made a trip to Germany. When they arrived at the little town where their family had resided and were well known, they were forced to leave. Westerners would say they were run out of town. As it turns out, their family had a history of horse thievery, stealing, and dishonesty of every sort. They were not welcome in their hometown.

As we continued, the Holy Spirit directed her to repent on behalf of her family and break any generational curse that was passed through her family lineage. She came to understand that this family curse (consequence) was still affecting her. It had robbed her financially, physically, emotionally, and mentally. She was reaping the consequences of sin and disobedience sown by her ancestors— some of whom she had never even met!

She then asked God to forgive her for any areas in her own life where she had given place to those same iniquities and had embraced ungodly belief systems and wrong thinking. She canceled any agreement with the enemy and came into agreement with God's Word, according to Philippians 4:19: "But my God shall supply your every need according to His riches in glory by Christ Jesus" (MEV). We prayed together and broke the curse of poverty and destruction that had been perpetuated through her family bloodline.

Within a few days this precious woman, full of gratitude, called us to report how God had already moved on her behalf. She never had to file bankruptcy. In fact, her business began to prosper immediately—it doubled and then tripled in profit within a few weeks! The accidents ceased, and her grandson was healed of the brain tumor. It has now been seven years since we prayed, and she continues to thrive. I must admit, this is one of the most amazing answers to prayer I have ever witnessed in that the transformation was so immediate and profound.

I make no claims to be an expert on the subject of generational iniquity and bloodline curses. Truthfully no one is! In fact, what I have learned throughout my years in freedom ministry is that there are no pat answers and the subject is inexhaustible. Despite this, we can rely upon the Holy Spirit to lead us into all truth, according to John 16:13:

> But when the Spirit of truth comes, He will guide you into all truth. For He will not speak on His own

authority. But He will speak whatever He hears, and
He will tell you things that are to come.

—MEV

I hope you are committed to finding freedom in Christ.
We were created by God to fulfill His purpose in our lives.
It is my prayer that the insights I communicate in this book
will help you navigate your own journey toward freedom.
I will share general principles with you, but only the Holy
Spirit can reveal the particulars of your own family history and how these truths apply to you. Therefore, ask
Him to reveal anything, past or present, that is hindering
you from experiencing the fullness of His good plans for
you. He is your wise and faithful guide, and He will help
you learn to live out and enjoy the freedom Jesus has provided for you.

ACTIVATION EXERCISE

In each chapter we will learn to connect with God on a
deeper level and hear His voice. Sometimes we think we
don't hear His voice, but Jesus said in John 10:27, "My sheep
hear My voice" (MEV). That means we may be hearing but
not recognizing His voice when He does speak. Scripture
tells us He speaks to us in our spirit, through His Word
(the Bible), through others prophetically, and through cre-
ation (Ps. 19:1; Rom. 1:20). Have no doubt: God will find a
way to speak to you.

Buckle your seat belts, friends! If you've never done
"hearing God exercises" before, you're in for the ride of
your life. As you complete these activation exercises, you
will begin to see life from God's perspective rather than
your own or what others have told you—or what the

enemy has told you. Knowing the truth will set you free and enable you to experience God at a new level.

Begin this activation exercise by finding a place where you can be alone, quiet your heart, and listen to God's voice. Then ask Him the following questions:

- o God, what are You saying to me personally through this chapter?

- o Are there foundations in my life that You want to rebuild?

- o Is there a heart attitude in me that You want to change?

Here is a prayer to help you get started in this activation.

Father, You are a God of truth. Open the eyes of my heart to see and hear Your truth in every area of my life. I give You permission to rebuild and restore those areas of my life that need Your touch. In Jesus's name, amen.

Chapter 2

CHARTING THE COURSE

W HEN I DISCUSS generational iniquity in freedom work-
shops and training sessions, people sometimes ask:
"Why do I need to consider or deal with generational
iniquity or bloodline curses? Let the past be the past! Why
should I dig up stuff that doesn't matter anymore? Didn't
Jesus die for all my sins? Wasn't all of this covered by the
blood of Jesus at the cross?"

The answer is a resounding yes! When Jesus died on the
cross, He became a curse for us. Galatians 3:13–14 clearly
states:

> Christ has redeemed us from the curse of the law by
> being made a curse for us—as it is written, "Cursed
> is everyone who hangs on a tree"—so that the
> blessing of Abraham might come on the Gentiles
> through Jesus Christ, that we might receive the
> promise of the Spirit through faith.
>
> —MEV

But it is important to remember that what Jesus provided by grace must be possessed by faith. Those gifts
include salvation and healing.

Salvation

Consider this: when we receive Christ as our Savior, our sins are forgiven and they are covered by the blood of Jesus. Notice that I said when we *receive*. Salvation requires an action on our part. We must appropriate what Jesus did for us. In other words salvation is available to us for the taking whenever we choose it. When we open our hearts and receive Christ by faith, we take ownership of what He has provided for us. We appropriate the shed blood of Jesus Christ, resulting in salvation. For "Everyone who calls on the name of the Lord shall be saved" (Rom. 10:13, MEV).

Jesus died to remove the penalty of our sins and failures. He liberated us from living in bondage to the curse that operates in the world as a result of sin. It is by His grace that we receive the benefits provided by His death and resurrection.

Healing for Our Bodies

Likewise, the payment for our physical healing has been provided through the suffering Jesus endured for our sake:

> Surely He has borne our griefs (sicknesses, weaknesses, and distresses) and carried our sorrows and pains [of punishment], yet we [ignorantly] considered Him stricken, smitten, and afflicted by God [as if with leprosy].
>
> But He was wounded for our transgressions, He was bruised for our guilt and iniquities; the chastisement [needful to obtain] peace and well-being

for us was upon Him, and with the stripes [that wounded] Him we are healed and made whole.
—ISAIAH 53:4–5, AMP

Jesus bore wounds on His back that we might be healed. However, we must receive what He did for us by faith to see healing manifest in our bodies. It is the same with our freedom from generational iniquity—we appropriate it by faith. How? When the Holy Spirit reveals truth, we repent and renounce our sins and the sins of our ancestors, and cast out any demonic influence. (That means we tell the demon it has no more authority and power in our lives, and it must leave. It loses its power and influence once the lies are exposed and truth is revealed.)

Often when individuals are released from a generational curse, they receive physical healing as a result—even when they are not specifically seeking physical healing. At other times people are released from a curse and the blockage to healing is removed, and then they can pray the prayer of faith and receive physical healing.

As I said earlier, there are no pat answers, formulas, or methods. One must be led by the Holy Spirit to find his personal pathway of healing. That involves inviting the presence of God and tuning in to hear His voice. As we intentionally connect with God, the Holy Spirit will reveal truth that we have no way of knowing apart from His showing us. God said in His Word, "Call to Me, and I will answer you, and show you great and mighty things which you do not know" (Jer. 33:3, MEV).

AM I RESPONSIBLE FOR THE SINS
OF MY ANCESTORS?

A question people often ask is, "Am I responsible for what my parents and ancestors did or the sins they committed?" No, we are not responsible for the sins of our parents or ancestors, only for our own sin. When I stand before God one day, I will be held accountable for my own relationship with Him. Romans 2:6 says, "God will repay each person according to what they have done."

In the following passage, sour grapes are used to illustrate the behaviors and character traits passed from one generation to another. This passage clearly tells us that we are responsible only for our own sin. While the New King James Version gives the more traditional translation, I have included the same passage from *The Message* Bible, which translates the text into today's language:

> In those days they shall say no more: "The fathers have eaten sour grapes, and the children's teeth are set on edge." But every one shall die for his own iniquity; every man who eats the sour grapes, his teeth shall be set on edge.
>
> —JEREMIAH 31:29–30, NKJV

> When that time comes you won't hear the old proverb anymore, Parents ate the green apples, their children got the stomachache. No, each person will pay for his own sin. You eat green apples, you're the one who gets sick.
>
> —JEREMIAH 31:29–30, THE MESSAGE

SINS OF THE FATHERS

Though we are responsible only for our own sin and not the sin of others, it is not uncommon for people to experience the consequences of their ancestors' sin through a bloodline curse. Perhaps you can identify an area of continual defeat in your life where the enemy continues to steal, kill, and destroy. Some examples might be poverty, addiction, repeated sickness and disease, barrenness—the list goes on. Ask yourself, "Do I see that same defeat in my family of origin?"

Jesus addressed the subject of generational iniquity with the religious leaders of His day. The Pharisees claimed that if they had lived in the days of their fathers, they would not have participated in the murdering of the prophets. Jesus said:

> Therefore you are witnesses against yourselves that you are sons of those who murdered the prophets. Fill up, then, the measure of your fathers' guilt.
> —MATTHEW 23:31–32, MEV

According to Jesus the religious leaders were hypocrites and spiritually blind. They claimed to surpass their fathers in righteousness while building monuments to the very prophets whom their fathers had murdered. Jesus knew they were plotting to kill Him and that the same murderous blood that ran through their forefathers' veins flowed through theirs as well. When Jesus was crucified, Pilate knew He was innocent. But Pilate violated his own conscience in order to please the religious leaders, who stirred up the crowd when they cried out, "Crucify Him!"

Exodus 20:3–6 tells us that the sins of the forefathers will be visited into the third and fourth generation of those who hate God. These religious leaders were their fathers' sons and bore the reproach of their fathers' iniquities that had not been repented of. A change of heart would have resulted in their blind eyes being opened to recognize and receive the Savior of the world.

Repentance Is the Key

The Greek word *metanoeo*, which is translated "repent," means to change one's mind and purpose as a result of knowledge or truth. (See Mark 1:15 and 2 Corinthians 12:21.) Repentance is not about just being sorry; it's a change of mind that results in an action.

The spiritual impact of our thoughts, choices, decisions, and actions is transmitted to successive generations. We can inherit a propensity to certain sins and weaknesses, and once we act upon them, they have an evil impact upon our lives. These sins and weaknesses also can potentially have a negative effect on our children and grandchildren.

According to brain researcher Caroline Leaf, PhD, "Science has shown how the thought networks pass through the sperm and the ova via DNA to the next four generations." But she says our thinking can change these generational patterns; the way we react to the events and circumstances in our lives—"our thinking and choosing—becomes the signal that activates or deactivates the generational issues in our lives."[1]

If we want to be free, we must first recognize any lies and wrong thought patterns we've embraced personally or inherited from our family of origin. Then we must repent and renew our minds according to the Word of God so we come into agreement with God's viewpoint. This will allow God to change our heart attitudes and set us free in the areas where we may have been held captive by our adversary, the devil.

Recently I was attending a book project review meeting with Bobby Williams, former executive director of Gateway Create Publishing. Bobby shared with me his excitement about the subject matter of this book. He understands how significant it is when individuals embrace the truth that their origins matter—that those beginnings have the potential of shaping their lives. Just before we ended the meeting, he shared a personal story with me, and I asked him for permission to share it with you. It is such a great example of how the Holy Spirit brings truth to families that liberates them to live in freedom and their true identity.

Bobby and his father were attending a men's conference in September of 2013. During the worship time, toward the end of the conference, Bobby noticed that he was feeling somewhat lighter. He said "things or burdens" that had been weighing him down were suddenly lifted from him. He couldn't figure out exactly why he was feeling so much lighter. The Holy Spirit spoke to Bobby, "Son, it's because your father has dealt with some family generational bondage during this conference, and that freedom is flowing to you." Bobby was the recipient of what Jesus referred to in Matthew 11:30: "For My yoke is easy, and My burden is light" (MEV).

My personal experience has been similar to Bobby's. But please don't misunderstand what I am saying. Just because freedom can sometimes come as a result of another person's repentance, that doesn't negate an individual's responsibility to repent for his own issues and bondage—of course he must do that as well. However, the closest analogy I can come up with is loosening the lid on a jar. The jar is easier to open once the lid has been loosened. In the same way, the freer I become, the more likely it is that my children and grandchildren will receive and experience freedom. My freedom flows to them, and then they have the opportunity to embrace that freedom for themselves. In addition, once you have tasted freedom, you have firsthand knowledge and understanding of how to pray and intercede for your children and grandchildren, and that increases their likelihood of receiving that freedom.

When family iniquities are not dealt with and repented of, each generation will usually become more extreme in repeating the weaknesses and behaviors of their forefathers. Everything reproduces after its own kind (Gen. 1:11). Chances are, the next generation will be "bent" or "twisted" in the same ways of the past. That weakness eventually becomes a bondage that has an evil effect in that family. Thank God the provision was made on the cross to restore us and our families to a blessed life! You could become the first in your family to make the decision to follow Christ and allow His Word to transform your thinking and ultimately your life.

BLESSINGS CAN BE OURS

The Scripture also tells us that blessings will flow from previous generations who love God and follow Him with their whole heart (Ps. 112). God's grace is always available.

Generational influence for evil is never a predetermined outcome for those who choose to follow after God and His ways. Notice in the following passage of Scripture how iniquity is linked to idolatry (an idol is anything we worship other than God) and that it concludes with the Lord extending mercy to those who love Him.

> You shall have no other gods before Me. You shall not make for yourself any graven idol, or any likeness of anything that is in heaven above, or that is in the earth beneath, or that is in the water below the earth. You shall not bow down to them or serve them; for I, the LORD your God, am a jealous God, visiting the iniquity of the fathers on the children to the third and fourth generation of them who hate Me, and showing lovingkindness to thousands of them who love Me and keep My commandments.
> —EXODUS 20:3–6, MEV

Jesus established that we, as partakers in the new covenant, are no longer subject to the judgment under the law of the old covenant. God has written His laws and commandments on the tablet of our hearts. As we live in fellowship with Him, we can live according to our new nature—Christ in us. The Apostle Paul wrote, "For God is working in you, giving you the desire and the power to do what pleases him" (Phil. 2:13, NLT).

As we delve deeper into the subject of generational iniquity, it's crucial that we grasp the enormous truth that if negative things are happening in our life, it's not because God is punishing us for our parents' mistakes. Do not believe the enemy's lies. God does not torture us. God does, however, want us to understand the generational tendencies that may be present in our family line, because He has provided a way out so we can enjoy the freedom Jesus died to give us. God has our best interests at heart—always! The Bible says:

> Christ has set us free to live a free life. So take your stand! Never again let anyone put a harness of slavery on you.
> —GALATIANS 5:1, THE MESSAGE

A FEW DEFINITIONS

Now let's take a look at several definitions that will help us better understand this issue of generational iniquity. Some of you will be familiar with these terms and others may be hearing them for the first time. Regardless, I encourage you to look over them carefully so there will be no misunderstanding or misconceptions as we move along in this book.

Generational sins

These are weaknesses and sinful tendencies inherited from our parents and family members. It is the attachment of our hearts to wrong things, not just wrong behavior. Idolatry, for instance, is anything we give first place in our lives other than God Himself, who deserves to be number one. Often we embrace the same sin patterns as previous generations and make them our own. A father may be an alcoholic but his son is a workaholic. The issue is the same but looks different. As these patterns are repeated throughout our lives, they eventually can affect our descendants in successive generations.

Sin

This means to "miss the mark" and is a general term for anything we do that causes us to fall short of the glory of God (Rom. 3:23).

Transgression

A transgression is a presumptuous sin. When we knowingly run a red light, tell a lie, or disregard authority, we are transgressing.

Generational iniquity

This refers to the way you are bent. One of the Hebrew words for iniquity is *avon,* which describes the crooked and perverse attitudes that originate with the fathers and are passed on to the children. It literally means "to bend or twist."[2] An iniquity involves inward motivation—an attitude or behavior that is more deeply rooted than a sin. It is a predisposition toward certain weaknesses. I've often heard generational iniquity compared to a tree that has endured harsh winds over a prolonged time. The winds will eventually bend or twist the tree, changing its appearance.

Generational patterns

These are patterns of thinking, actions, beliefs, behaviors, and habits that we have inherited from our immediate family or relatives. When we live under the constant example and influence of these patterns, it usually follows that we will repeat them in our own life.

Legal right

When a person sins, a door is opened to the enemy, giving him a *legal right* (or permission) to trespass. In other words he has been invited in and has a right to be there. Until that sin has been repented of, the legal right remains. In ministry situations, we always look for legal rights when we pray for people. The enemy can be given legal rights when we come into agreement with something in opposition to God's Word. In other words, when we believe a lie.

A great practical example of a legal right is when we open the door of our home to a visitor. If we invite someone into our home, they have a right to be there. If we close the door and they enter against our will or force their way in, they are in violation of the law and our rights. In the spiritual realm, repentance is the key to breaking a legal right. When we repent, we appropriate what Christ has done, and the enemy must leave.

Bless

To be blessed is to be empowered to succeed. Blessings are favor or gifts bestowed by God. We will dig deeper into the subject of blessings in chapter 4, "Empowered to Succeed."

Curse

A curse causes failure anywhere it is functioning in a person's life. In chapter 5, "Destined for Failure," we will discover more about the working of a curse in the lives of individuals and families.

Proverbs 26:2 tells us that "a curse without cause will not alight [land]" (MEV). That simply means there must be a reason—a cause—for a curse (evil effect) to be present. A curse can manifest:

o   As a consequence of sin and disobedience

o   As a result of words we have believed that were spoken by someone in authority

(usually a parent or a person of significant influence in our lives)

- When we make pronouncements over ourselves by coming into agreement with the enemy through our own self-talk (telling ourselves, for example, "I'm so stupid," "I'll never be a success," "I always get sick during flu season," etc.)

Bloodline curses

These come through our family of origin as a result of sins our relatives committed. We choose whether or not to embrace that sin, but we may struggle with that weakness or bent regardless. If our ancestors embraced sin and did not repent, a door was opened and legal right, or permission, was given for a bloodline curse to operate. This term can sometimes sound mystical, but it isn't. If someone leaves a door open where invaders can easily access your home, then someone needs to close it, whether you or a family member opened the door. Repentance is the key to freedom.

Inner vows and judgments

These are usually negative determinations made in reaction to a circumstance or an event. It can be a verbal or nonverbal judgment of the heart. Inner vow and judgment statements usually begin with "I will never," or "I always." An inner vow is a negative thing because it means we are trying to control an area of our life rather than submitting to or trusting in God.

Repentance

This means to change one's mind. It is about turning away from sin and wrong thinking and turning to God. It is a change of mind that results in a change of action. (See Luke 3:8–14; Acts 3:19; and Acts 26:20.)

Identificational repentance

Very often a person will recognize a destructive force over themselves and their family that is the result of the sin of a previous generation. Sometimes the individuals who are responsible for the iniquity that produced the curse (consequence) are no longer living, or they are alive but unrepentant. Some may even be God haters.

According to Scripture, we have the awesome privilege of standing in the gap through identificational repentance. Perhaps the best example of this is recorded in the Book of Nehemiah. When Nehemiah heard of the negative condition of his home country, he recognized that the sin of his forefathers had brought a curse over the land. The Israelites had rebuilt the temple, but the gates around the city were still destroyed and needed rebuilding. Although Nehemiah had no part in what his ancestors did, this was the heartfelt prayer of repentance he spoke on behalf of himself and his forefathers:

> Let Your ear now be attentive, and Your eyes open, that You may hear the prayer of Your servant, which I now pray before You, day and night, for the children of Israel Your servants, and confess the sins of the children of Israel, which we have sinned against You. Both my father's house and I have sinned. We have acted very corruptly against You and have not obeyed the commandments, nor the statutes, nor

the judgments, which You commanded Your servant Moses.

Please remember the word that You commanded Your servant Moses, saying, "If you behave unfaithfully, then I will scatter you among the nations, but if you return to Me and keep My commandments and do them, though your outcasts are under the farthest part of the heavens, I will gather them from there and bring them back to the place where I have chosen to establish My name."

—Nehemiah 1:6–9, mev

God responded to this prayer by empowering the Israelites to rebuild the walls in fifty-two days.

Renounce

To renounce is to give up claim to something. It means to put aside voluntarily. When we renounce something spiritually, we give up any claim that particular sin or iniquity occupies in our heart. We let it go and allow a divine exchange—that is, God replaces darkness with light and good for evil. In place of fear, we experience His love. He gives us joy to replace sadness and depression.

Break

To break is to dissolve, annul, or destroy. Breaking a curse and breaking the power of the enemy over our lives is essential in the Christian walk. We have been given authority over the works of the enemy, and we experience freedom as we come out of agreement with the enemy's lies and into agreement with God and His Word. Luke 10:19 tells us, "Behold, I give unto you power to tread on serpents and scorpions, and over all the power of the enemy: and nothing shall by any means hurt you" (KJV).

Idolatry

This is anything we worship other than the one and only true God. It includes those things that occupy our heart: whatever we give our time, money, and attention to more than God Himself. Idolatry can include worship of idols or excessive devotion to anything. We commit idolatry when we give anyone or anything what God alone deserves. (See 1 Corinthians 10:14; Galatians 5:19–21; Romans 1:24–25; Exodus 20:2–6; Deuteronomy 4:15–18; and Jeremiah 10:3–5.)

The Blessed Life

I want to live the blessed life and experience all God has for me. That kind of life is possible when we choose to deal with generational iniquity. But what does a blessed life look like? Psalm 112 describes the blessings God promises to His people. One translation calls this psalm "The Blessed State of the Righteous" while another gives it the title "God's Covenant of Mercy." The following is a summary of the blessings promised in Psalm 112 to the those who fear the Lord and delights in His commandments.

- o Their descendants will be mighty on the earth.

- o Wealth and riches will be in their houses.

- o Their righteousness will endure forever.

- o They will be a light in the darkness.

- They are gracious, full of compassion, and righteous.

- They deal graciously and lend.

- They will guide their affairs with discretion.

- They will never be shaken.

- They will always be remembered.

- They will not be afraid of evil.

- Their hearts are steadfast, trusting in the Lord.

- Their hearts are established.

- They will not be afraid.

- They will give to the poor.

- Their horn (strength) will be exalted with honor.

- The wicked will see these things and be grieved—and disappear!

I don't know about you, but this is exciting stuff for me! I want to experience these blessings for my family and for myself. I desire to live a blessed life that is totally devoted to God so that I can receive His love without any hindrance and live life to the fullest. I want to enjoy my life! After all, we can be saved and go to heaven, yet still experience hell on earth. I want to know God's presence and experience His kingdom right now in this life.

Now that we have considered some of the basics, in the next chapter we will look at some biblical examples of generational patterns. No doubt you'll easily recognize the same patterns as being alive and well in our culture today. But first, spend some time meditating on what we've discussed in this chapter.

ACTIVATION EXERCISE

Get quiet before God and ask Him the following questions:

- o Is there an area of defeat in my life that also existed in my family of origin?

- o Would You identify any lies or wrong thought patterns that I have embraced personally or inherited (passed down) from my family?

As He shows you the truth, come into agreement with God. Let this prayer guide you in beginning this activation:

Jesus, You came to set the captives free. Help me to renew my mind and line up with Your thinking. I choose to come into agreement with Your Word and see life from Your perspective. In Jesus's name, amen.

Chapter 3

BIBLICAL PATTERNS OF GENERATIONAL INIQUITY

GREW UP BEING taught Bible stories in Sunday school and later read them to my children when they were growing up. I loved hearing about the remarkable faith of the men and women in God's history book and the magnificent victories they won over their enemies, such as when David defeated the Philistine giant, Goliath. I was convinced I could never measure up to these heroes and heroines of faith. Because we rarely talked about their struggles, I never gave much thought to their weaknesses. In my mind, they were clearly superior to any of us, and their victories stood far above anything a common believer could ever attain. I placed them on a pedestal along with all the pastors, preachers, and evangelists in our particular denomination.

In contrast the Apostle Paul emphasized that it is just as important to learn from the failures of God's people that are recorded in the Bible as it is to admire their faith. Their mistakes provide valuable lessons. Paul said, "These things happened to them as examples for us. They were written down to warn us who live at the end of the age" (1 Cor. 10:11, NLT).

The truth is, the men and women of the Bible were just like you and me. They experienced personal battles that revealed their strengths and weaknesses. Therefore, we can benefit from studying their lives to gain insight on how to avoid their mistakes and learn their strategies for success.

A number of years ago while driving my children to school I heard an announcement over the radio that a well-known televangelist had fallen into immorality. I remember the shock and disappointment I felt. How could this happen? Without even thinking, I heard myself break into a hymn I sang as a child: "On Christ the solid Rock I stand. All other ground is sinking sand."[1] In that moment, God was ministering a truth to my heart: man will fail you, but God never does.

Unfortunately some people are disillusioned with the church because of the failures of some leaders. In their minds, ministers' credibility has been lost. Obviously the church is not perfect—not even close! Leaders should have a higher level of accountability because of the office to which God has called them. (And despite popular opinion, there are far more who maintain good character, high morals, and impeccable integrity than not.) But God has chosen His children, with all their imperfections, to draw people to Himself. Jesus gave His life for that purpose. He said, "And if I be lifted up from the earth, I will draw all men to Myself" (John 12:32, MEV).

As the saying goes, God doesn't choose the qualified. He qualifies the chosen.

Through the ages, men and women have consistently been mightily used of God, but none are without flaws, limitations, and deficiencies. Many have fallen into gross sin, while others have stayed the course and left an astounding legacy of faith. Still others have failed but then risen again to finish well. I have an intense desire to "finish well," and I fully intend to pursue that end. However, I know I will accomplish this only by God's grace as I continue to pursue Him.

David, a Man After God's Heart

Perhaps no single Bible figure gives us more generational ammunition to work with than David. Despite all his failings, he was called a man after God's own heart (Acts 13:22). This was uttered by God Himself, no less! David certainly had his good points. He had charisma like no other. He was an intelligent, dynamic leader and trainer of men; a mighty warrior, handsome dude, and gifted poet and musician. But most of all, David was quick to repent and devoted to God.

David's sin with Bathsheba was no worse than yours or mine. We may not have committed adultery and had someone killed to cover our sin, but we all have feet of clay. Can you even imagine having your story—both the good and bad—written in the Bible for all to read and examine throughout the centuries all over the world? David's life has been scrutinized in seminary classes and books; even Hollywood movies have exploited his shortcomings.

Despite his amazing qualities and his commitment to God, which moved the Father's heart, David did sow a lot of bad seed. The Apostle Paul tells us that we reap all kinds of death (consequences) when we sin. He wrote, "The wages of sin is death; but the gift of God is eternal life through Jesus Christ our Lord" (Rom. 6:23, KJV).

We see evidence in Scripture that David was a "hands off" kind of dad. He was so busy with his wives, concubines, political exploits, and battles, there was little time for the kids. On many occasions, David responded passively rather than proactively to situations involving his children. A tragic example was when his daughter Tamar was raped. David did nothing about it! (See 2 Samuel 13.) This lack of paternal leadership provoked anger and resentment in some of his sons, and they reacted by rebelling against their father. In contrast, David invested significant time teaching and training his son Solomon to pursue wisdom. Solomon himself tells us this throughout the Book of Proverbs. (See Proverbs 3 and Proverbs 4:4–7, for example.)

It seems like a fair conclusion that David's failings as a father stemmed from the painful things he experienced as a son. I'm convinced that David functioned from a root of rejection, judging from the story recorded in 1 Samuel 16. God sent the prophet Samuel to the house of David's father, Jesse, to anoint one of his sons to be the next king. Jesse presented seven of his sons to Samuel as possible candidates for the job but never once thought to include David. After those seven were eliminated, Samuel inquired if there were any other sons. Jesse's response went something like this: "Oh yeah, there's the youngest one—the keeper of the sheep." *Hello!* I don't know about you, but I would have felt pretty unimportant and unloved. David probably felt more like a servant to Jesse than a son.

When David later became king, he committed adultery with Bathsheba and then committed murder to get her husband out of his way. She must have been one fine-looking woman for him to go to such great lengths to pursue her and risk his reputation to satisfy his lust.

God told David he wouldn't be the one to build a temple for Him, though God commended him for his desire to do so. Some theologians believe God didn't allow David to build the temple because he had so much blood on his hands, for he was a mighty warrior. Others think it just wasn't David's gift and calling to build the temple, so God chose Solomon to complete that project instead.

In David's lifetime he opened the door to sexual sin, murder, and violence (2 Sam. 12:1–24). He also established life patterns that would continue for generations. Although David's sons were gifted and talented men, they followed in some of the sin patterns of their father. Let's take a look at some of the pitfalls and heart attitudes that led to their demise.

DAVID'S SONS: SOLOMON, ABSALOM, AND AMNON

Solomon

The son of King David and Bathsheba, Solomon is renowned in the Old Testament for his wisdom. Early on, Solomon knew his need for God. When he became king of the united kingdom of Judah and Israel, young Solomon asked God to help him rule his people well and with great wisdom. (Remember, Proverbs 4:1 and 7 lets us know his father had impressed upon him that getting wisdom is "the principal thing.") True humility is recognizing our need for God. God was pleased with Solomon because he didn't ask selfishly for wealth and a long life. God answered his humble prayer for wisdom but also gave him longevity and riches to boot—the two things most of us desire, if we are honest. And He blessed Solomon to build the famous temple in Jerusalem, which became his crowning achievement.

It was said of Solomon that he, like his father, had a weakness for women. He was a handsome man with great wisdom, but his pursuit of foreign women, who worshipped idols, eventually led his heart away from God. Scripture says Solomon had seven hundred wives of royal birth and three hundred concubines.

Unfortunately, in time Solomon felt he no longer needed God's protection when he imported chariots and horses for military security. Solomon also exported weapons so that he could acquire silver and gold. All of this was forbidden in the Law. As recorded in 1 Kings, Solomon's idolatry sent Israel into deeper idolatry and violence. Idolatry is the root of all sin whether the idol is money, lust, or anything else. An idol is anything that replaces God in our hearts. A regular heart check is imperative for the people of God.

Amnon

This was David's firstborn son from his wife Ahinoam the Jezreelitess (2 Sam. 3:2). Amnon was first in line for the throne of Israel. But he took what didn't belong to him, just as his father had done. He longed so much for Tamar, his half-sister, that he became lovesick. Tamar was a virgin and ready for marriage, which made it even more difficult for him since marriage between a half-brother and sister was forbidden by the Law of Moses.

The Bible tells us that Amnon forced himself on Tamar, disgraced her, and then hated her, demonstrating that it was lust, not love, motivating his actions. Her very presence was a reminder of his foolish sin, and he wanted her out of his sight. Even today it is common for a relative to reject the one he or she has abused. Amnon's lust for women was carried out in a violent, incestuous way (2 Sam. 13:10–19). Amnon built upon the example of his father, David, and took his sexual sin even further.

Absalom

This was David's son by Maacah, daughter of Talmai, king of Geshur (2 Sam. 3:3). Evidently he had his father's looks and charm. He was easy on the eyes, as some would say. He stole the hearts of the people of Israel through his fine looks, stature, and charisma. But Absalom took David's sin to a new level. He committed political adultery with the nation when he attempted to usurp his father's throne and erected a monument to himself. Absalom did not have a good end, as you can read in 2 Samuel 18. After Absalom's tragic end, King David mourned deeply for his son. He must have felt tremendous regret.

A youth pastor once told me that children will often take sin of their parents one step further. Obviously, this doesn't always happen, and we always hope it won't; nevertheless, I've seen this time and again. The enemy finds weak points in families and that's where he strikes. David's family is a prime example of sinful heart attitudes being transmitted to children, causing immeasurable pain and suffering for them, for David, and for their nation. Clearly we can see in David's life the importance of dealing with all of our heart attitudes and behaviors that can lead to dysfunction in families.

ABRAHAM, THE MAN OF GREAT FAITH

Abraham, Isaac, and Jacob were fathers of the faith; nevertheless, they had generational weaknesses of deceit. Abraham lied just to save his own skin when he claimed that his wife, Sarah, was really his sister. His fear for his own life put hers in jeopardy not just once but on two separate occasions (Gen. 12 and 20). Notice how the root of fear was the motivation for lying and deceitfulness.

Fear will cause you to do things you wouldn't normally do—things completely out of character. You can never make wise decisions if they are motivated by or filtered through fear. To illustrate this, let's look at David again. When David was running from Saul, afraid for his life, he decided to go to the land of the Philistines. The story is told in 1 Samuel 21. So why would David choose to run to the land of the Philistines, Israel's enemy? Gath was the hometown of their military hero, Goliath—the giant David had killed and then beheaded. David's irrational decision to flee there put him in a dangerous situation. To escape death, he resorted to desperate measures. Scripture says he feigned madness and let saliva run down his beard. Most of us think of David as being a fearless warrior, and in many ways he was. But fear will cause you to do things that make no sense, even to the point of humiliating yourself!

Just as in David's lineage, we see Abraham passing down the negative traits not to one generation but to two.

Isaac, Abraham's son

Abraham's son, Isaac, walked in his father's steps. His wife, Rebekah, was a beautiful woman; therefore, Isaac was terrified that the men of Gerar would kill him in order to take her for their own. In a painful replay of his father's behavior, Isaac pretended that Rebekah was his sister in order to save his own skin. Once again, the root of fear produced the fruit of deception. However, the story turned out all right, as you can read in Genesis 26. But isn't it amazing how family patterns of behavior can create identical scenarios?

Jacob, Abraham's grandson

Many of you know the story of Isaac's son, Jacob, who plotted with his mother, Rebekah, to steal his older brother Esau's birthright. Jacob, like his father and grandfather, had trouble trusting God to work things out. At times he schemed, lied, and manipulated to get what he wanted. Later in his life, after an all-night wrestling match between Jacob and God, the Lord gave him a new name: Israel, meaning "he struggles with God, and prevails." (See Genesis 32:24–32.) During that encounter, the Lord touched Jacob's hip, and from that day forward he walked with a limp. The result was that Jacob, the former manipulator, learned how to surrender control and trust God.

Through the years I've heard various leaders say, "Don't trust anyone who doesn't walk with a limp." I agree that there is a positive brokenness that must take place in the heart of a leader in order for him to walk in true humility. This shapes him into the sort of person others want to follow. That was the case with Jacob. After his personal encounter with God, he became a new man with a new identity.

RAHAB THE HARLOT

Rahab, surprisingly, is one of the two women named in Hebrews 11 as examples of godly faith. Why in the world would God include a former harlot among His faithful saints? Because God demonstrates His mercy and power against the backdrop of human weakness. The power of God transformed Rahab from a pagan harlot into a woman strong in faith. Her story is recorded in Joshua chapter 2.

When Joshua and his men used Rahab's house in Jericho to hide their spies, they were entering into miracle territory. God sent them to the only resident of Jericho who resolved to fear and obey Israel's God. If a common harlot of Canaan could turn from her old lifestyle, courageously help God's people (putting her own life at risk), and end up in the lineage of Jesus, then surely nothing is impossible with God! Her story is an encouragement to us all.

Rahab's life demonstrates how choosing to follow God changes generational iniquity into generational blessing. Rahab married Salmon, the son of Judah's tribal leader. Their son, Boaz, married Ruth, and then Ruth and Boaz had Obed, who became the father of Jesse, King David's father. Jesus, the Savior of the world, was David's descendant. Therefore, Rahab was a mother in the line of the Messiah. This story is a true indicator that our past, no matter how immoral and corrupt, doesn't have to determine our future.

Timothy

A great New Testament example of a strong Christian heritage is the Apostle Paul's travelling companion, Timothy. Paul wrote to Timothy of the positive influence of his upbringing and the importance of his childhood instruction in the Word of God:

> I am reminded of your sincere faith, which first lived in your grandmother Lois and in your mother Eunice and, I am persuaded, now lives in you also.
>
> —2 Timothy 1:5

> But continue in the things that you have learned and have been assured of, knowing those from whom you have learned them, and that since childhood you have known the Holy Scriptures, which are able to make you wise unto salvation through the faith that is in Christ Jesus.
>
> —2 Timothy 3:14–15, mev

Timothy's mother and grandmother raised him in the faith. His soul was grounded through studying the Scriptures, and that prepared him to become an apostle of the church and bishop of Ephesus. Thanks to Timothy's excellent training by two amazing women, he became a gift to the church and a true servant to Paul. He helped Paul to preach the "good news" and was instrumental in starting many Christian congregations. Timothy struggled with timidity but overcame it. He learned that through Christ all things are possible.

Many of God's chosen leaders in the Bible had troubled backgrounds. Perhaps you do too. Maybe you have inherited negative family traits and characteristics, or you struggle due to poor choices your family members made. Or maybe your own choices have resulted in severe or unfortunate consequences. Regardless, Jesus has already paid the price for your freedom from every form of the curse (Gal. 3:13). And as you allow His power to work in your soul, it will break the negative cycles and shatter those chains of bondage. Not only will you be free, but also you can stop that generational iniquity from being passed on to your children and grandchildren. Just as Rahab did, you can build a better future for your children.

ACTIVATION EXERCISE

Now let's move toward action that will change our lives forever. I urge you to get alone, quiet your heart, and ask God to show you things you have no way of knowing unless He reveals them to you (Jer. 33:3). Ask the Lord:

- o Is there anything You want me to know about my family heritage? What traits are good and beneficial? Which characteristics are unhealthy and damaging?

- o Have I allowed anything to displace You from being first in my heart?

- o Following You changes generational iniquity into generational blessings. Is there an area of my life where I'm not following You fully?

After you've let the Lord speak to you concerning those questions, spend some time in prayer. Here is one to help get you started:

Lord, I want You to be first in my life. Forgive me and my family of origin for allowing other things to take Your place in our hearts. I bring _____ (what has taken God's place) to the cross and I ask You to replace it with Your truth and presence. Empower me to follow You fully. I break any demonic power that has held me captive, and I receive Your forgiveness and freedom. In Jesus's name I pray, amen.

Chapter 4

EMPOWERED TO SUCCEED

WHY DO SOME people succeed and others do not? Have you noticed that it seems as if whatever some people touch turns to gold? I believe with all my heart that God fervently desires to bless His people (and He does that every day of our lives!). But does that mean if you follow God you will be rich, healthy, and never have another problem? Absolutely not! We live in a fallen world where bad things happen to good people and good things happen to bad people. It rains on the just and unjust (Matt. 5:45). But generally speaking, I believe when we follow God and align ourselves with His will and purpose for our lives, we then live in the palm of His hand. Therefore, we can trust that all things will ultimately work together for our good (Rom. 8:28).

As we seek God with all our heart, we won't rely upon our own understanding. Instead, we will acknowledge Him in the way we think and in all our decisions, and then He will bring the desires of our hearts to pass in His timing (Prov. 3:5). How do we align our hearts with God's will for us? We begin to think like He thinks and to believe what He says about us. The Bible calls this the renewing of our mind.

Do not be conformed to this world, but be transformed by the renewing of your mind, that you may prove what is the good and acceptable and perfect will of God.

—ROMANS 12:2, MEV

For the weapons of our warfare are not carnal, but mighty through God to the pulling down of strongholds, casting down imaginations and every high thing that exalts itself against *the knowledge of God*, bringing every thought into captivity to the obedience of Christ.

—2 CORINTHIANS 10:4–5, MEV,
EMPHASIS ADDED

In other words we put aside "stinkin' thinking"! We identify and "capture" every thought that does not agree with the Word of God, and we throw that thought out and replace it with the truth. The more time we spend with God in His Word, the better we will get to know Him and the better we will be able to identify wrong thinking. Jesus said He came to show us what our heavenly Father is like because He, the Son, would only say and do what the Father was saying and doing (John 14:8–10).

Our flesh (carnal nature) naturally wants to conform to the negative thought patterns of the world (Rom. 8:6). However, in this book we are exploring another factor at work: not all of your thought patterns originated with you.

Dr. James Richards says we are wired for success but programmed for failure.[1] This can be the result of wrong thinking that has been passed down for generations. The good news is that when we learn what God says in His Word and choose to believe and trust Him, we come into agreement with His definition of success. As a result, we will experience the blessings He has for us. Some of us will be the first in our families to embrace God's will and purpose. That means we can begin a new spiritual legacy that will bless generations to come. We and our families will be blessed, which means to be empowered to succeed.

What Is Success?

God told Joshua: "Keep this Book of the Law always on your lips; meditate on it day and night, so that you may be careful to do everything written in it. Then you will be prosperous and successful" (Josh. 1:8).

Most people define success in terms of acquiring wealth and achieving goals, status, power, and favor. They view success as the key to the "good life": being admired, financially safe, emotionally secure, and able to enjoy the fruit of their labor. For them, success is about the here and now. Even in some churches success is often determined by numbers, size, dollars, and prestige rather than spiritual maturity and godly influence.

God describes success in terms of faithfulness and obedience. He desires a close relationship with us that inspires and cultivates our loyalty and devotion. He wants us to think of success in terms of who we were created to be—which then impacts how we live! God's Word has much to say about how our thought patterns and actions impact our success. For instance, Proverbs 16:3 says, "Roll your works upon the Lord [commit and trust them wholly to Him; He will cause your thoughts to become agreeable to His will, and] so shall your plans be established and succeed" (AMP).

I am convinced that when we are walking in God's purpose, living with our heart connected with His, we can love what we do, even though we may go through seasons of training and waiting for God to unfold His plans for our destiny. What we do becomes an expression of who we are in Him. Author Oswald Chambers is quoted as saying, "God's call is for you to be His loyal friend, to accomplish His purposes and goals for your life."[2]

PREPARING FOR BLESSING

When we lived in California, I knew a family who appeared to be immune to trouble. The entire family was healthy and extremely prosperous in every way: physically, socially, emotionally, and relationally. They had great attitudes and exercised wisdom in decision making. "Positivity" must have been one of their top five strengths!

I must admit that I felt a little jealous—not because I wanted them to go through adversity, but because I wanted our family to experience the blessings they enjoyed. I understood that no one is immune to having problems and at some point they probably would as well. But the degree of health this family enjoyed was so rare.

As I learned more about them, I discovered that they had a long legacy of relatives who had loved and served God. Their families of origin were extremely generous, loving, and encouraging. This family seemed to be reaping the benefits of that godly lineage.

There is something to be said for families who have faithfully served the living God for generations. Blessings follow obedience, and negative consequences follow disobedience. Whether for good or bad, invisible forces are at work that have the potential to determine the destiny of individuals and families.

Jesus Christ purchased our freedom from the curse of sin when He died on the cross. He triumphed over sin and every evil power (Col. 2:14–15), which means we no longer have to live under the slavery of generational iniquity. That's the good news of the gospel. If you are the first one in your family to become a Christian, then you have the opportunity to pioneer a new legacy of blessing for your descendants.

However, even in believing homes there are often issues that have been hiding under the surface for centuries. Because those things have never been addressed, the freedom Christ purchased has never been appropriated in certain areas. The challenge when communicating this truth is that those who are suffering or experiencing trouble could feel condemned or criticized. They might think the reason they haven't experienced freedom from generational bondage is because they personally have done something wrong. I want to make it perfectly clear that's not what I am saying. It is possible that person has done something to open a door to the enemy, but that is not necessarily the case. In John 16:33, Jesus said that in this world we will have troubles and tribulations, but that we can rejoice in the midst of it all because *He* has overcome the world!

In my own case (and maybe yours also), some bad seeds were sown by previous generations that have affected the way my family thinks and responds to life situations. Those seeds have influenced our ability (or inability) to receive the blessing Jesus died for us to have. We are still in the process of seeing a reversal of the consequences of bad choices and wrong thinking in our family line. We're now choosing to sow good seed that will produce good fruit in our lifetime and in the generations to come.

I want to clarify that my family members sowed a lot of good seed. In fact, they sowed more good than bad—without question! I owe my Christian heritage to my family. I come from a long line of men and women who loved God and served Him faithfully. I was brought up to know and love God. As I mentioned in chapter 1, most of us inherit both good and bad from our families of origin.

Understanding what Scripture says about blessings and curses and how they affect your life will give you a whole new perspective on the various issues you and your family members may be experiencing. I believe this revelation will help you to unlock and overcome the problems that have seemed unresolvable, frustrating, and exhausting.

HEARING GOD'S VOICE

The first step in learning to receive the blessing God has already provided is to practice the presence of God and tune in to His voice. Nothing compares to hearing God's voice for yourself. God longs to converse with you whether you hear His voice Spirit to spirit, through Scripture, prophetically through others, or by some other means. Hearing the voice of God is key to experiencing His blessing.

John 10:27 says, "My sheep hear My voice...and they follow Me" (MEV). Sometimes we hear but don't follow. That is rebellion or "going our own way." Other times we don't hear God's voice because we are so preoccupied by the busyness of this world. We either don't take time to listen, or we simply ignore warning signals that would bring blessing to our lives. This is a vital point that bears repeating: we are designed for relationship with God, and He longs to have fellowship with us. It's never too late to start spending quality time with God.

I knew a young woman who left her home one night to meet some of her friends. As she touched the handle of the car door, she heard, "Don't go." She hesitated, then again heard, "Don't go." She chose to ignore the warning. Looking back, she now knows the Holy Spirit was clearly speaking to her to stay home. Evidently, she had ingested a couple of glasses of wine before leaving home. That night she had a fender bender and was arrested and charged with DUI. She was thrown into the county jail with drunks, prostitutes, and drug abusers—a world that was foreign to her. In addition to being scared half out of her wits, she received a violation on her record that wouldn't be lifted for years to come. She was also given a hefty fine that crippled her financially for months. The event ultimately changed her for the good, but it could have been avoided. What a stiff price to pay! Surely there was an easier way for her to learn to pay attention to God's voice than having to experience jail time! Many times I've heard her say, "If only I had listened and obeyed."

BRING ON THE BLESSINGS!

In Deuteronomy 28:3–13, Moses outlines the blessings that are available to God's children who walk in obedience to Him:

> You will be blessed in the city and blessed in the country. The fruit of your womb will be blessed,

and the crops of your land and the young of your livestock—the calves of your herds and the lambs of your flocks. Your basket and your kneading trough will be blessed. You will be blessed when you come in and blessed when you go out. The LORD will grant that the enemies who rise up against you will be defeated before you. They will come at you from one direction but flee from you in seven.

The LORD will send a blessing on your barns and on everything you put your hand to. The LORD your God will bless you in the land he is giving you. The LORD will establish you as his holy people, as he promised you on oath, if you keep the commands of the LORD your God and walk in obedience to him. Then all the peoples on earth will see that you are called by the name of the LORD, and they will fear you. The LORD will grant you abundant prosperity—in the fruit of your womb, the young of your livestock and the crops of your ground—in the land he swore to your ancestors to give you.

The LORD will open the heavens, the storehouse of his bounty, to send rain on your land in season and to bless all the work of your hands. You will lend to many nations but will borrow from none. The LORD will make you the head, not the tail. If you pay attention to the commands of the LORD your God that I give you this day and carefully follow them, you will always be at the top, never at the bottom.

This passage is rich with God's promises to those who are faithful to Him, and I urge you to diligently study it. Prayerfully ask the Holy Spirit to reveal His truths as you meditate on the Word. In the meantime, I have put together a summary of the content of these passages for you to review. Let the promises of God germinate in your heart.

Favor

This is the demonstration of God's presence in your life. Exodus 33:16 says, "How will anyone know that you look favorably on me—on me and on your people—if you don't go with us? For your presence among us sets your people and me apart from all other people on the earth" (NLT). Proverbs 3:4 also tells us that if we obey God's commands, "Then you will find favor and much success in the sight of God and humanity" (GW).

Prosperity

Deuteronomy 30:15 says, "See, I set before you today life and prosperity, death and destruction." Choosing God's ways produces blessing and peace. Scripture tells us that when a man's ways are pleasing to the Lord, even his enemies will be at peace with him (Prov. 16:7).

Fruitfulness

After God created Adam and Eve, the first thing He did was bless them, and then He told them, "Be fruitful, and multiply, and replenish the earth, and subdue it: and have dominion over the fish of the sea, and over the fowl of the air, and over every living thing that moveth upon the earth" (Gen. 1:28, KJV). The blessing of fruitfulness applies to any area in which a person wants to see reproduction occur—in their talents, family, livestock, crops, business, etc.

Victory over our enemies

God promised His people, "I will contend with those who contend with you, and your children I will save" (Isa. 49:25).

Health

Proverbs 3:7–8 tell us, "Do not be wise in your own eyes; fear the LORD and depart from evil. It will be health to your body, and strength to your bones" (MEV). Today we know that much stress makes our bodies sick. Living in the peace of God and obedience to His Word brings life, health, and wholeness to us—spirit, soul, and body. That doesn't mean we never experience sickness and disease, because we live in a fallen world. But we can avoid many of the illnesses that can be attributed to stress.

Exaltation

Psalm 37:34 says, "Wait on the LORD, and keep His way, and He shall exalt you to inherit the land; when the wicked are cut off, you shall see it" (NKJV). The word *exalt* means to lift or raise up. Those who follow God and trust Him are recipients of His exaltation. Scripture also tells us that as we humble ourselves under the mighty hand of God, He will exalt us.

Peace

We read in Psalm 37:11, "But the meek will inherit the land and enjoy peace and prosperity." Those who are meek put their trust in God rather than themselves. They enjoy the blessing of casting their cares on Him and resting in His love and provision for their daily needs. Meekness doesn't indicate weakness but strength under control. God is the owner of the earth (Ps. 24). Those who obey Christ become children of God (Gal. 3:27) and joint heirs with the Lord (Rom. 8:17). This manifests through peace and provision of our daily needs.

As Moses concludes this list of blessings, he uses two visuals that I have used in prayer many times to invoke God's blessings in various situations. He says, "The LORD will make you the head and not the tail; you shall be above *only* and not be beneath" (Deut. 28:13, NKJV, emphasis added). There's something about that verse that excites me and catapults me forward in believing God for His blessing.

One of the ways that we are "the head and not the tail" is related to lending versus borrowing. I don't want to owe anything to anyone. I want to be a giver. For years I prayed, "Lord, allow me to be the lender and not the borrower." He has answered those prayers and helped me to help those in need or those who can't help themselves on many occasions. It truly is more blessed to give than to receive, although in my opinion you have to be a good receiver to be a good giver! It's good to know how it feels to be on both ends. It gives you a whole new perspective, and it keeps you humble and aware of your need for God.

At times when I feel defeated by circumstances and "under it," so to speak, I remember Psalm 8:6, which tells me God has given me dominion. So my challenging situations are to be put "under my feet"—not on top of me, weighing me down. In other words, the trials we face are not to rule over us and control our lives—even when things appear hopeless or impossible from a human perspective. We can choose to look to God for help and trust His Word. This is a true exercise of stretching your spiritual muscles when going through hard times, but the reward is worth it.

ACTIVATION EXERCISE

Are you experiencing God's blessings today? Are you the head and not the tail? Are you above *only* and not beneath? I encourage you to quiet your heart and work through the following activation as you study Deuteronomy 28:3–13. Then pray the prayer provided as you listen and allow His Spirit to bring fresh revelation and insight.

- Ask the Holy Spirit to show you the areas where you are currently receiving His blessings. Then thank Him for those blessings.

- Ask the Lord, "Is there an area where I'm not receiving Your blessing? Is this true of my family of origin as well?"

- Ask, "Is there something You would have me do in response?" (For example, does He want you to ask for blessing, repent, forgive, open your heart to receive, close any open doors the enemy has used to invade any area of your life, etc.?)

I have provided the following prayer as a model to get you started as you respond to the areas where you are not experiencing His blessing. However, you will want to personalize your prayer to be as specific as possible. Designate whether it is the maternal or paternal side of your family that you are addressing. Talk to God about the identifiable negative traits, involvements, sins, and iniquity you have observed in your family. Also, name the demonic spirit (or describe its function) that has empowered the sin or iniquity, and then take authority over it in the name of Jesus Christ. (Some examples are spirits of hate, fear, heaviness, infirmity, sexual perversion or lust, bondage, jealousy, pride, error, divination, antichrist, stupor or spiritual blindness, etc.) Ask God to replace that spirit with the opposite spirit (love, courage, freedom, health, purity, kindness, goodness, self-control, etc.).

Remember, you are talking to God! He knows your every thought and action. Talk to Him like you would a good father—from your heart. You can't do it wrong! Ask for His insights and thoughts into your life and your family. Learn to be comfortable in His presence and allow Him to speak to you like a son or daughter.

My husband used to say, "There's no such thing as a bad prayer!" Don't hold back if you experience a release of emotions. Let go of your hurts, frustrations, inhibitions, and anything you have kept shut up inside—maybe for a lifetime. If a dam breaks inside, let the tears flow. Shed those heavy spiritual weights, and your heart will be light. Open your heart to love God and allow Him to love you, and then thank Him for what He's done.

> *Heavenly Father, I want to be a recipient of Your blessings. I want to follow You completely with my heart. I ask Your forgiveness for _____ (name any area of rebellion or disobedience). I receive Your forgiveness and ask You to cleanse my heart of any wrong attitudes and reveal any wrong patterns I have formed as a result.*
>
> *I ask Your forgiveness also on behalf of my family of origin who made wrong decisions and choices _____ (name them specifically). I ask You to release me also from the consequences*

of their sins. According to 2 Corinthians 5:17, I declare that since I belong to You, Jesus, I am a new creature; old things are passed away and all things have become new in my life. I break every demonic hold over me and my family. I believe that when You died on the cross, You took upon Yourself every curse that could ever come upon me. Today I receive and appropriate what You finished. I choose to walk in obedience to You, Lord, and receive Your blessings and the gift of Your presence in my life. I want to leave a good heritage and legacy to my children and all of my future descendants. I pray this in Your name, Jesus, amen.

Chapter 5

DESTINED FOR FAILURE?

OW MANY TIMES have you asked yourself: "Why does this always happen to me?" "What is wrong with me?" "Why is there never enough?" "Why don't I ever feel fulfilled?" And the list goes on. Does having these questions mean you are destined to fail? Absolutely not! These are questions that demand answers. Because knowing the truth makes you free, you need truthful answers to the questions that plague your thought life.

Have you believed lies about yourself, God, or others? Have you made an inner vow (i.e., "I will never..." or "I always...") that puts you in the driver's seat of your life and sabotages your trust in God? Or maybe you are dealing with a generational curse (consequence) that didn't have its origin with you. Regardless, you need answers.

In this chapter we will focus on both individual and generational curses; however, I want to emphasize that when bad things happen, you are not always dealing with a curse. We have already established that a curse is a consequence of sin that brings failure and frustration in our lives. It is the opposite of the blessing Jesus secured for us on the cross.

In chapter 2 we discussed how Jesus became a curse for us. We are new creations in Him. When we receive Christ,

He gives us a new heart and we have His mind—our spirit can think His thoughts. Sin, sickness, disease, and continual poverty are not our inheritance. But let's face it: the enemy will utilize every device, every weakness, and every opportunity to rob us of those blessings. He is merciless! He never has a compassionate day. He never says, "I think I'll go easy on them today." It just doesn't happen! We must know our authority in Christ, line up our thoughts, words, and beliefs with the Word of God, and close the door to every demonic spirit, whether generational or not.

Finally we must absolutely refuse to allow our adversary to steal our inheritance and devour our destiny. Scripture tells us:

> Be sober [self-controlled] and watchful, because your adversary the devil walks around as a roaring lion, seeking whom he may devour.
> —1 PETER 5:8, MEV

Deuteronomy 28:15–68 lists several curses that will fall on those who are disobedient to God's ways. I encourage you to prayerfully study these curses and ask the Holy Spirit to show you anything you need to know about you or your family history. Whether the curse came through spoken words, willful disobedience, or from our ancestors through bloodline curses, the results of curses can be broken. We experience our freedom in Christ when we come out of agreement with the evil that will lead us to destruction and into agreement with God. He wants His children to enjoy the abundant life Jesus sacrificed Himself for us to enjoy.

If there is a vicious cycle in your life that was also evident in your family, it would be beneficial to find out why that pattern exists. To summarize Deuteronomy 28:15–68, those living under a curse often experience defeat, failure, oppression, family breakdown, barrenness, unfruitfulness, poverty, humiliation, and chronic mental and physical sickness, just to name a few. Please understand that everyone who experiences one of these issues is not necessarily under a curse or consequence of sin. However, when you experience them over and over in a chronic and persistent way, it's a good idea to do some soul searching and ask the Holy Spirit for revelation.

THREE TYPES OF CURSES

Scripture speaks of several kinds of curses that fall on the disobedient. In the next several pages I want to focus on three types of curses that often affect our lives.

Generational bloodline curses

These result from unrepentant sin committed by ourselves or our ancestors. When someone sins and does not repent (change his or her thinking) and turn from his own way, a door is opened to a curse (consequence). That door remains open in a family bloodline until someone makes a decision to repent and declare: "This sin and iniquity stops here with me!" We have the awesome privilege of "standing in the gap" and repenting on behalf of our ancestors, according to Leviticus 26:39–42.

An example of a bloodline curse is found in Genesis 4. In this passage, both Cain and Abel brought offerings to the Lord. The Bible tells us that God was pleased with Abel's sacrifice but not with Cain's. We know Cain had a serious anger-management problem and became jealous of his brother. His jealousy and hatred drove him to murder Abel.

Scripture records God's conversation with Cain: "Then the Lord said to Cain, "Why are you angry? Why is your face downcast? If you do what is right, will you not be accepted? But if you do not do what is right, sin is crouching at your door; it desires to have you, but you must rule over it" (Gen. 4:6–7).

Cain evidently gave an unacceptable offering, and even more important, he had given it with a wrong attitude. God offered him opportunity to repent. God always offers a way of escape. But Cain refused to repent and received severe consequences for his sin as a result.

> And then He said, "What have you done? The voice of your brother's blood is crying out to Me from the ground. Now you are cursed from the ground which opened its mouth to receive your brother's blood from your hand. From now on when you till the ground, it will not yield for you its best. You will be a fugitive and a wanderer on the earth."
> —Genesis 4:10–12, mev

Sin caused Cain to lose his profession as a farmer and become a wanderer. And he was sent away from the presence of the Lord. Even after we accept Christ, sin can still separate us from God—not because He turns us away, but because our own guilt and shame hinders us from coming boldly into His presence.

Biblical records show six generations of Cain's descendants who gradually degenerated in their moral and spiritual condition until they became completely corrupt. Eventually God sent a deluge of water to prevent the final triumph of evil.

As I read this sad and senseless story, I often think about how it all would have ended quite differently if Cain had repented. I also wonder what would have happened if Cain's descendants had responded to God and turned from their wicked ways, beginning a lineage of obedient lovers of God.

Frequently I have watched individuals and families move from defeat to victory once they recognize the way their lives have paralleled those of previous generations. When they repent and embrace God's truth and His ways, the curses are broken and situations are reversed from death to life. Later in this chapter, I will show you some ways to determine whether this kind of trouble is operating in your life.

Curses from words

In one of our ministry staff meetings, my pastor, Robert Morris, said this: "Regularly I pray for Gateway Church and against any word curses that have been spoken over us." This is such wisdom. Curses are spoken all the time for one reason or another. People may be jealous, envious, or angry at us. There are a multitude of reasons people say evil or negative words over institutions, churches, businesses—and people! Satanic cults consider it their assignment to speak curses over churches and individuals they view as a threat to their agenda. We must not be ignorant of the enemy's devices, as 2 Corinthians 2:11 instructs. And remember, Proverbs 26:2 tells us that "a curse without cause shall not alight" (NKJV).

Since we are not perfect, at times we may open doors to the enemy's attacks through the words we speak, unforgiveness, prayerlessness, giving place to fear, and so on. Prayer provides added protection and deliverance from the enemy's schemes. The enemy waits for an opportune time, when our defenses are down, to gain entry. He tried it with Jesus (Luke 4:13), and he will try it with us.

Even after all these years in ministry, I am still amazed at the crippling effect mere words can have when spoken over a person's life. When I was in grade school, I remember hearing the kids say, "Sticks and stones can break your bones, but words can never hurt you." That is absolutely untrue. Words can be destructive or constructive, and they can definitely hurt you. James wrote, "And so blessing and cursing come pouring out of the same mouth. Surely, my brothers and sisters, this is not right!" (James 3:10, NLT).

My young grandson once had a teacher call him an idiot simply because he couldn't answer a question she posed to the class. That young, impressionable nine-year-old boy believed her words and embraced that belief for many years. Those words hung over him like a dark cloud and almost cost him his God-given destiny. This is a typical example of a word curse. He truly believed he was an idiot! I still remember the day God revealed to him the effects that event had on him. We prayed together and broke the curse of the words his teacher spoke over him. We asked the Holy Spirit to show him the truth. He heard the Lord whisper in his spirit, "You have My mind." God replaced the lie with truth—and it set him free! When you hear and believe the voice of God, it brings freedom.

Negative words such as "You will never amount to anything" or "You're no good!" have the potential of producing a prophetic outcome over an individual. Many parents have uttered the words "You're dumb" or "Don't be so stupid" over a child in a moment of frustration. Sometimes hurtful or destructive words are spoken by someone in authority (i.e., teachers, coaches, or spiritual leaders) and can have an impact on that individual for years to come. Such words can even set in motion harmful effects that impact generation after generation. They contain spiritual power to shape belief systems, and their lingering effect will remain until someone recognizes it and applies the truth of God's Word.

I once ministered to a woman in her fifties who was convinced she was stupid and incapable of learning new things. That belief system began when she was a little first-grader. Her father helped her with homework, and when she didn't get a problem right, he would hit the table and tell her how stupid she was. Those words defined her as she grew into adulthood, and stunted her ability to learn and succeed. Her belief system did not change until she embraced the truth that she was not stupid and consciously broke her agreement with the lie her father spoke. She had to believe what God says about her—the she has the mind of Christ (1 Cor. 2:16). What happened to this tiny, sensitive little girl substantiates the words of Proverbs 23:7, "For as he [or she] thinks in his [or her] heart, so is he [or she]" (NKJV).

Consider the words God spoke over His Son, Jesus, when John baptized Him in the Jordan River: "This is my Son, whom I love; with him I am well pleased" (Matt. 3:17). Those are life-giving words! Granted, there are times as parents when we are not well pleased with our children. But keep in mind that your words have power, and you are either speaking life or death over your children. Perhaps your words won't result in a physical death, but negative words can lead to the death of their hopes, dreams, and future successes. If your child receives the things you say into their soul, those words will shape their destiny.

Failure can be the result of negative words taken to heart. This can be especially true of children, who don't have the ability to process thoughts and their effects in the same way as adults. Even adults who do have that ability often struggle with words spoken over them. They unconsciously believe them, whether they are true or lies.

Your own words can sometimes be even more destructive than what others say about you. They can become self-fulfilling prophecies. Growing up, I remember times when I would do or say something foolish. Under my breath, I would utter words such as, "You are so stupid! Why did you do (or say) that?" After a while, you begin to believe those harsh self-judgments—so be careful what you speak about yourself! The Bible tells us, "You are snared by the words of your mouth; you are taken by the words of your mouth" (Prov. 6:2, NKJV).

Curses from disobedience

The Bible tells us:

> The curse of the LORD is on the house of the wicked, but He blesses the home of the just.
> —PROVERBS 3:33, NKJV

> Cursed is the man who trusts in man and makes his flesh his strength, whose heart departs from the LORD.
> —JEREMIAH 17:5, NKJV

As these verses attest, obedience activates blessings, and disobedience usually results in negative consequences, including death, according to Romans 6:23.

Sometimes the origin of misfortune or trouble is not directly related to previous generations. Instead, it can be the result of your own wrong choices, actions, or events that have taken place during your life. Or you may have done things that perpetuated the curses or difficulty that originated in previous generations. Often our soul is predisposed toward the sins that were weaknesses for our ancestors. Or perhaps you saw your parents, grandparents, or aunts and uncles live out those sinful choices before you. Whatever the case, remember that we always have the ability to choose God's ways. It can just be more difficult when those ancestral tendencies are in the genes (and possibly fueled by demonic power).

Living in obedience simply means to live according to God's Word. We are wired for relationship with our loving heavenly Father. And the closer we get to Him, the more we will want to obey—because we love Him. When we disobey, God doesn't raise His hand to slap us; He withdraws His hand to allow us to choose—to give us free will. When we choose to disobey, there is always a consequence. I can't drive this home enough: Bad things don't happen in life because God is punishing you for your ancestors' sin. Sin, once it is initiated by us or someone in our lineage, opens the door for the enemy to perpetuate destruction. God in His mercy wants to show you a way out—a better way that brings His favorable results in your life. God wants your heart!

Seven Indicators of a Curse

Before you can break a generational curse, you must recognize that it exists! What does it look like? The following seven indicators will help you identify if you are dealing with a curse. Ask the Holy Spirit to give you revelation as you ponder these possibilities. Remember, if you are dealing with one of these symptoms in your life, that does not automatically mean you are dealing with a curse.

For example, a woman can have trouble conceiving a child, but that doesn't necessarily mean there is a generational curse at work in her life. However, it is a possibility to consider and pray about. I knew a woman who was unable to conceive because of a vow she made as a teenager: "I will never have children when I grow up." When she repented and broke her agreement with the words she had spoken, she conceived a baby in a short period of time. In this case, the woman had cursed herself. But there can also be physical reasons a woman is unable to conceive. In that case, prayer for healing is needed.

In these matters we must hear the voice of God. Remember, we are no longer subject to these curses if we are in Christ. However, in order to experience the freedom we have through Christ, we must receive what Jesus did for us on the cross and appropriate our inheritance of blessing under the new covenant.

Here are seven indicators to look for in your family line to determine whether a curse may be at work in your life:

1. **Mental and emotional breakdown.** If you have a family history of confusion, deep depression, an extremely anxious mind, and insanity, a curse may be at work (Deut. 28:20, 28, 34, 65). Involvement in the occult is often at the root of mental and emotional torment.

2. **Repeated or chronic sickness,** especially when hereditary. A pattern of wasting diseases, severe burning fevers, inflammations, boils, tumors, scabs, sores, incurable itches, blindness, and serious and prolonged sickness or disease may be a sign of a curse (Deut. 28:22, 27, 35, 59–61).

3. **Barrenness, tendency to miscarry, or chronic female problems.** An inability to conceive, debilitating menstrual cramps, irregular periods, failure to menstruate, frigidity, cysts, tumors or growths, and structural defects connected with the reproductive process may be the result of a curse on the "fruit of your body" (Deut. 28:18, NKJV).

4. **Breakdown of marriage and family alienation**, especially if hereditary. This type of curse is described in Deuteronomy 28:41, "You shall beget sons and daughters, but they shall not be yours; for they shall go into captivity" (NKJV). Rebellion, pornography, sex, drugs, satanism, and the occult are often at the root of this curse.

5. **Chronic financial insufficiency**. If you can't get ahead, are always behind financially, or never have enough, and this has been a pattern in your family, you might be dealing with a curse. See Deuteronomy 28:17, 29, 38–40, 47–48.

6. **Being accident-prone** can often be an indicator of a curse, although Deuteronomy doesn't specifically list it. Those who have repeated accidents or "freak" accidents often are experiencing a curse that needs to be broken.

7. **Suicides and untimely deaths**. The Bible talks about the destruction of not only individuals but also entire families. People under this curse seem to have a sense of knowing that something is going to happen. They may have even bought into a lie that they will die young for one reason or another—because their father died young, or what have you. Some would call it a death wish. This is negative faith—embracing death instead of life.

Now that we have established ways of identifying the possibility of a generational curse, here are some possible open doors that have allowed the curse to operate:

- Worshipping or acknowledging false gods

- Occult involvement

- Dishonoring parents

- Injustice, mistreatment, or oppression of the helpless

- Illicit or unnatural sex

- Legalism, carnality, or apostasy

- Anti-Semitism

- Theft or perjury

- Withholding the tithe or other material resources from God

- Words spoken by people with relational authority (father, mother, husband, wife, teacher, priest, pastor, coach, etc.)

- Oaths or pledges that bind people to ungodly associations

- Curses that proceed from servants (worshippers) of Satan

- Self-imposed curses

There are many other curses listed in the Bible. These curses can appear harsh unless you realize they are consequences of disobedience to God. Remember, God is not the one who curses us. A curse is simply the acquired result of choices made in deliberate opposition to what God instructs in His Word. Consider this illustration.

If a father tells his child not to go into the street for safety reasons, and the child does the opposite, the consequence may be that the child is hit by a car. The father didn't cause the accident. The father, out of love for the child's safety, warned him to protect him. If the child had disobeyed and wasn't harmed, the father may have given him a consequence, such as not allowing him to play in the front yard anymore. Or the child may get a swat on the behind to make a lasting impression of the danger. We must consider the Father's heart by comparing His discipline to that of a healthy earthly father who disciplines with love and the child's best interests at heart.

When a person practices certain sins (sexual sin, violence, idolatry, prejudice, anti-Semitism, racism, witchcraft, fear, etc.), they become deeply ingrained or iniquities (weaknesses toward certain behaviors). When those behaviors are practiced repeatedly (allowing Satan to gain control of the mind, will, and emotions), that behavior will begin to control not only the individual but also future generations. The result is a generational curse.

Keep in mind that under the new covenant we are no longer under the Law, and forgiveness is ours the moment we ask. However, it is important to understand the cracks the enemy uses to try and get in to rob us of the blessings that God has for us.

ACTIVATION EXERCISE

The word *curse* appears in Scripture 230 times, so it most definitely is not a subject to ignore or to fear. Curses are not mystical, as they are sometimes presented, but simply the result or consequence of sin. As we appropriate the finished work of Christ through repentance, we can experience freedom. We are to possess by faith what Jesus accomplished by grace.

I encourage you to find a quiet, undisturbed place to still your heart before God. Connect your heart to His and inquire whether or not you might be dealing with a curse—generational or otherwise.

- o First, identify the iniquity. Ask the Lord, "Is there a curse (consequence) working in my life? What is it? What is the origin? When did it first take root in my life?"

- o Repent of the sin and iniquity. Come into agreement with what God says. Ask God to forgive you and to forgive your family (maternal and/or paternal side) for opening those doors of destruction.

- o Renounce (give up or put aside) involvement and participation in the sin on behalf of yourself and those in your family who participated.

- o Break the power of the enemy—past, present, and future!

- o Now, pray this prayer and remember to be specific in identifying family lies and belief systems that are in opposition to God's Word and truth:

Thank You, Lord, for helping me understand that You are a good God and Your desire is that Your children be blessed. When You went to the cross, You took the consequences of every sin I have committed or would ever commit. I appropriate those blessings today and break every curse over me and my family. I open my heart to receive Your blessings, and I repent on behalf of myself and my family of origin for any door that was opened to the enemy to rob me of my inheritance. I break the enemy's power over my life. In Jesus's precious name I pray, amen.

As we continue, I think you will enjoy some of the stories of people who received freedom from generational iniquity. I hope their examples will help give you more understanding of how to connect the dots between the past and the present as you pursue your pathway of deliverance.

Chapter 6

FAMILY FINANCIAL BAGGAGE

A LL FAMILIES HAVE baggage of some sort, and mine was no different. My late husband, Jim, and I both brought plenty of baggage into our marriage. Unfortunately some of our spiritual baggage caused financial destruction for years. We eventually realized that we were struggling with and being defeated by a family curse—for thirty-five years, to be exact.

I must emphasize here that every financial problem people face or poor decision they make is not necessarily demonically influenced. Oftentimes it is the result of poor stewardship and/or failure to obey God's Word in the area of tithing and giving.

Our story is a noteworthy one, and I'll do my best to recall the details accurately. I've shared it many times when I speak, and I never cease to be amazed at how many people identify with our journey on some level. As you read about the financial calamities that occurred, you will notice that most of them were due to bizarre circumstances beyond our control. The world may call it "bad luck," but events like these may strongly indicate that some kind of curse is operating. We discovered that a generational curse was, indeed, at the root of our problems— and I think you'll agree.

Never Enough

My husband was a well-educated and bright aeronautical engineer with years of experience in his field. Yet no matter how much money he made, we could never seem to get ahead. There was never enough. If we needed a thousand dollars, we had only five hundred; or if we required five thousand, we had one thousand. Even after I went back to work and received a substantial salary, there still wasn't enough to cover expenses. Something would always happen to drain our bank accounts. I once compared our financial situation to pouring money into a sieve—it just seemed to disappear.

Through the years I noticed people who were able to take nice vacations with their families and afford things we couldn't. Those folks often made far less money than we did. Because we were good stewards of our money, it never made sense. I must admit that I felt jealous and couldn't help but notice the reality of what was happening. I wanted my family to enjoy nice things too. But the bondage of financial debt so often stood in the way.

A Strange Cycle Begins

From the beginning of our marriage we incurred debt as a result of a very unusual circumstance. Jim realized someone had taken his credit cards and maxed them out. So we began working with credit card companies, but we were never able to clear up the theft completely. As a result we struggled to pay off a lot of debt that we didn't incur. Jim and I did have credit cards for emergencies, but we seldom used them.

Meanwhile God was progressively showing us the truths that would lead us to financial freedom. I recall the first teaching on tithing that Jim ever heard after he began his walk with God. He came home after church one Sunday, got out his Bible, and searched out all the scriptures concerning what the pastor had taught. After he completed his research, he looked up at me and said, "Yep, he was right. That's what the Bible says." Jim wrote his first tithe check that day and never missed paying our tithes from then on, even when things got really tough for us financially!

In those early years Jim was in the building business. He was severely tested when that first tithe check happened to be 10 percent of the profits on a house he had just built and sold. It was a significant amount—especially considering that he was new to all this. Yet he wrote out the check and never looked back.

About seven years later Jim lost his building business because Fannie Mae was not lending. My husband had buyers wanting to purchase the houses he had built, but they couldn't get loans to buy them. After exhausting all our resources, we ended up moving to California so Jim could get back into the aeronautical field. At this point we were $100,000 in debt, I might add. Keep in mind that this was in the seventies, so that amount was even more staggering than it is today! Somehow we were able to pay off the debt in just one year. Our CPA assured us that what happened to us couldn't be verified on paper. He couldn't determine how we did it! We were living in miracle territory.

Notice how, even though the enemy would try to steal from us, the Lord was faithful to step in and save us. To quote Charles Dickens, "It was the best of times, it was the worst of times!" We realized later that by leading us to California in the midst of Fannie Mae not lending to us, the Lord had worked for our good. He directed us to The Church on the Way to be trained and discipled by Pastor Jack Hayford, who I believe is one of the great Christian leaders of our day.

LEARNING TO GIVE AND THE JOY OF RECEIVING

Pastor Jack is an excellent Bible teacher who taught us well on the subject of giving. Jim and I also did further study together on tithing and giving offerings, and we were faithful to put what we learned into practice. This included practicing being led by the Holy Spirit in giving offerings to missions, building programs, individuals in need—whatever God put on our hearts.

I share all this to emphasize that the financial troubles we experienced were not due to a lack of obedience in the area of giving. In fact, we often emptied our checking account to help others in need. We learned to live by faith. Those are days I wouldn't trade—despite the financial struggles. It was wonderful to be part of someone else's financial miracle.

For instance, during our early days of living in California, we befriended a young couple who was attending seminary. We didn't know it at the time, but they were several hundred dollars short of having enough money to pay their rent. God put on our heart to give them money. We didn't know why we were to give them the money, but we both heard God very clearly on the amount. We sent the money anonymously to their home mailbox so they wouldn't know who had given it.

We later heard how the story played out. The very day their rent was due, the wife told her Jewish landlady (who was actually an atheist) that they didn't have enough money for rent; however, she knew that her God would supply it before the day was over. The landlady, knowing her tenant was a Christian, laughed at her in disbelief. Later that day, the wife visited her mailbox and opened it while the unbelieving woman stood nearby. She pulled out the money and laughed as she handed it to her landlady, saying, "See, I knew the Lord would provide." She got the last grin.

What a blessing that was to see God work in the lives of those precious people—and we got to be a part of it! And what a thrill to know that Jewish woman had witnessed a miracle. These kinds of experiences were regular occurrences in the early days of our Spirit-led walk. It is so faith-building when we review the things that God has done in our lives.

Although we struggled in our finances, it was evident that God honored our giving, because we received gifts and favor in the midst of it all. We never missed paying our bills on time, no matter how bad things got. I remember a short time before I went back to work, our mortgage was due and we didn't have the full amount. In California, mortgage payments are usually three times what they are in Texas—not that the size or the amount is ever an issue for God! Nevertheless, it was a lot of money. Without us saying a word, my parents sent a gift to cover that month's mortgage and the one to come as well. They just wanted to bless us. They had no idea what a timely blessing it was!

Floods and Rainbows

The next chapter in our California years was when we moved to the San Fernando Valley to be closer to church, work, and our daughter's school. Little did we know that another catastrophe was headed our way. Due to the tremendous rains in the Los Angeles area, lakes were overflowing, and the dams released water to keep them from spilling over their banks. When that happened, the water flooded our home as well as several of our neighbors' homes. We lost a lot of our keepsakes along with our car, carpets, and more. Among those keepsakes was Jim's Marine trunk and his Purple Heart. Every pot and pan we owned was filled with mud and debris. Once again we were forced to borrow money to make all the repairs, and purchase a new car and other necessities.

Jim and I fought back the tears as we watched the pastors and staff of our church shovel mud from our driveway and pull the wet carpet out of our home. We'd never felt so devastated...and yet so loved! They put us up in a nice apartment until we could get on our feet. The support was overwhelming, as were the financial gifts we received to help with expenses.

One afternoon we were looking out the bedroom window into what had been our incredibly gorgeous backyard. It had been filled with all kinds of plants and flowers (including over fifteen long-stem rosebushes in every color). There were fruit trees and every berry imaginable. The floodwaters had destroyed everything, covering it with mud and debris. Yet suddenly there appeared a beautiful rainbow that was contained between the fences that ran on the east and west boundaries of our backyard!

A friend was there visiting us and said, "Linda, God is saying through the rainbow that this will never happen to you again." And it didn't! Even though the dam released water several times after that, it would crest around our porch but never entered our front door again as we prayed and believed God for a miracle. There was no human explanation for why the floodwater didn't come into our home.

Our lives changed dramatically after the flood. You guessed it—we incurred debt once again. But we were not the same people as before the flood. The enemy definitely caused a setback for us financially, but the changes in our hearts couldn't be measured in dollars. What the enemy meant for harm, God worked for our good (Gen. 50:20, Rom. 8:28). He gave us beauty for ashes! Here is how the prophet Isaiah expressed it:

> When the enemy comes in[,] like a flood, the Spirit of the LORD will lift up a standard against him.
> —ISAIAH 59:19, NKJV

Here's an interesting side note: Pastor Hayford once pointed out, regarding Isaiah 59:19, that in the original Hebrew, commas were placed in the sentence as displayed above. Therefore, the meaning is that God "like a flood" raises a standard. It is not saying the enemy comes in "like a flood" as we've often been taught. The enemy had intended a literal flood to steal our finances and destroy our property, but God raised up His people to flood us with His love and to give us practical support.

PROPHETIC PRAYER

Up to that point, we hadn't shared our concerns with anyone other than a few friends at church. We would occasionally ask for prayer for provision of one thing or another. But after the flood episode, my husband and I eventually confided to our friend, who was a pastor, some of our financial struggles. As we recounted our story to him, he got a visual of a pipeline that went back as far as he could see. He felt that it prophetically represented something that had been passed through the generations through my husband's bloodline. The enemy had used this pipeline to steal from us and destroy us financially.

Our pastor-friend sensed that there had been some kind of dishonest financial dealing that went far back in my husband's ancestral lineage. My husband prayed and repented on behalf of himself and his family. He believed the curse had been broken off of our finances. Then we claimed God's promise to those who tithe:

> "And I will rebuke the devourer for your sakes, so that he will not destroy the fruit of your ground, nor shall the vine fail to bear fruit for you in the field," says the LORD of hosts.
>
> —MALACHI 3:11, NKJV

We believed God and continued to be faithful in our giving. Afterward, things definitely improved in our finances. However, I always sensed that there was more work to be done and that we had simply scratched the surface of the issue.

The Move That Never Happened...and Those That Did

In 1987, exactly seven years after the flood, my husband received a promotion that would require our family to move to Atlanta from Los Angeles. I flew to Atlanta and worked with a builder to construct a beautiful home in a wooded area of Marietta, Georgia. The land was breathtakingly beautiful with rolling hills, tall trees, and creeks that ran across the backyards of the Southern style homes. Our home in Los Angeles sold in a fairly short period of time, and we were on our way.

Then the bottom dropped out! Due to military cutbacks, the navy cancelled the contract with the aeronautical company where my husband was employed. My husband's promotion and our move to Atlanta were cancelled as well. And we were left holding the bag. We lost our down payment on the Atlanta home and had to search for another home to buy in Los Angeles, since our previous one had already sold. Once again, we incurred tremendous debt in the process.

The end result of that catastrophe turned out to be profitable, though it left us emotionally drained. We were able to get into a fabulous townhome rental with tons of amenities while we had a new home built. That home overlooked the Angeles National Forest and offered an interesting view of the hang gliders who hovered over our backyard as they soared from the nearby hills down into the canyons. And there were cute little critters everywhere on our property!

We lived in that house for a little less than three years; then Jim retired, and we decided to move back to Texas to live closer to our extended family. We just happened to buy and sell at exactly the right time, since the price we received for our home was over a third more than we paid for it. That's California real estate—but that's also the God we serve. Once again, our heavenly Father came through for us! And we were on our way back home to Texas.

The profit we made from our California home put us in a good financial position for a fresh start in Texas. So it looked like our financial troubles were finally over. Nevertheless, as time went on, the financial calamities continued. Although we certainly did not do everything perfectly, the majority of our debt continued to be caused by bizarre circumstances that were not our fault. I do believe we received an element of freedom when my husband repented and broke the generational curse that our friend had seen in the vision. However, sometimes there are additional pieces of the puzzle to reckon with.

THE IRS SCARE

Shortly after our move back to Texas, we received an alarming letter in the mail claiming that we owed the IRS thousands of dollars. We were shaken! We couldn't get anyone on the phone who would talk any sense to us. This allegation apparently came from the City of San Francisco, and we couldn't figure out what they were talking about. We knew it wasn't our debt, but there was no convincing the IRS of that. We felt defenseless and were concerned that they would take our home. After exhausting our resources, Jim and I decided to fast and pray for three days.

During the fast, a good friend from California called to check in on us and see if we were getting settled into our new home. I mentioned our situation to her. As it turns out, she had recently heard a Christian IRS executive being interviewed on a Christian radio station in Los Angeles. He now dedicated his time to helping people who were having issues with the IRS that they couldn't resolve on their own. My friend called the radio station and got the man's contact information for me.

I immediately called the IRS expert. He spent about a half hour on the phone with me, and then sent me his book and some brochures to guide me through the process of clearing up the mess. Evidently there are some specific ways to successfully deal with the IRS that the average person doesn't know about. His materials were amazingly helpful. It took several months, but we eventually cleared up the mistake. This could have been devastating to us had the Lord not intervened by connecting us with this incredible man. Trusting God in our finances became our middle name!

THE FAMILY BUSINESS

Within a year of returning to Texas after my husband's retirement from the aeronautical industry, we opened a family photography business. We incorporated all our family's talents. Our oldest daughter was a gifted photographer, and our youngest became our makeup artist to assist our customers in looking their best for their portraits. We even sent her to California to be trained by a leading television makeup artist. Jim handled the business side of things while I ran the front desk and the marketing side of things.

A few days before we were to open, I took a bad fall and ended up in the hospital for a week. Then I was in physical therapy for almost a year. I crushed my tibia plateau, which required bone grafting and extensive surgery to restore the leg. Jim and the girls had to go it alone, and my responsibilities pretty much got put on hold. Neglect of our marketing portion was the clincher. We offered a great product, but marketing is everything in that kind of business, and we were functioning on word-of-mouth alone.

We were able to hang on for a while but finally realized there was little hope. We were worn out from the long hours, and none of us had taken a salary from the business since it began. To top it off, my father died suddenly of a massive heart attack, and we put everything on hold. My dad passed away in July, we lost Jim's brother in August, and his mother died in September of the same year. The business was just a small part of all the grieving our family had in store.

By this time our oldest daughter had become engaged and wanted to focus on her upcoming marriage and starting a family. Our youngest daughter decided to pursue her nursing degree. Neither was interested in continuing the business. While we were excited for both of them to pursue their life dreams, the business had come to a screeching halt. It was obvious that the venture was over. At one point we thought a large chain photography company would buy the business, but they reneged at the last minute.

Once again we walked away with tremendous debt and disappointment. We had prayed and sought counsel before taking on this endeavor. What in the world happened?

Yet again a force was working against us to bring death and destruction to our finances. This venture left us with debt that required us to mortgage our home, which would have been paid off that year. We also had to pay off the Small Business Association loans acquired to help fund the business.

Looking back, we probably should have never started that business. There were warning signs, such as the statistics of failure in that kind of industry, and the timing wasn't good. Regardless of who or what was to blame, more financial destruction took place. I knew the enemy was at least responsible for part of the failure. My bizarre fall should never have happened. That was the last straw for me.

I Got Mad

Have you ever heard of righteous indignation? That's what I experienced after the previous series of events—especially the last one! I felt something wasn't right or fair, and I felt righteous anger that I'd never experienced before. I knew in my heart that God was not the author of the hellishness we were experiencing, so I decided to fight. I began with fasting and prayer. That prayer turned into warfare prayer, where I took my authority in Christ! There was a point when I knew I had broken through in prayer and something was going to be finalized—a true victory. There was no physical evidence that what I was sensing was true, but I knew it spiritually in my "knower." I felt a breakthrough was imminent.

I visited a local bookstore that same afternoon. As I browsed the various sections, I somehow ended up in the business and financial section. I never go there! My eyes were drawn to the very top shelf—it was supernatural. I spotted a book that said *Death in Debt*. I got a ladder, took the book from the shelf, bought it, and headed home. The book was written by a Christian author named C. S. Lovett, and you can't even find it today. I know very little about the author and remember less about the book. I just know that God used it to speak to me.

I saw the phrase "Death in Debt" and knew God was giving me revelation. I had never thought of a death spirit in relation to finances, although it makes complete sense. When God encouraged His people to "choose life" (Deut. 30:19), that life was associated with the blessings He offered, which included financial prosperity. The "death" was on the side of the curse—and poverty and debt were listed there.

LAYING THE AX TO THE ROOT

When Jim got home that evening, I shared the day's findings about the death-in-debt spirit, and together we began praying. The root of our financial woes was finally revealed when we recognized a seven-year debt cycle that had repeatedly played out over a span of at least thirty-five years. Obviously this type of cycle is a little harder to detect due to the fact that it transpires over a long period of time. The question was, how could this destructive cycle have operated in the lives of two believers who put God first in their finances by tithing and giving offerings? We earnestly asked for insight and counsel from the Lord.

In earlier years there had been prayers of repentance and prophetic words related to the generational iniquity of financial dishonesty that our pastor-friend had seen. As I said, we did experience a certain level of freedom after addressing that. However, we had not dealt with the spirit assigned to our finances that was at the root of the seven-year debt cycle. God revealed to us that some of our ancestors had belonged to a secret society that required its members to take vows that pronounced curses and ruin over their descendants should any try to leave their society. Only God could have shown us this truth! We learned that God's seven-year cycle (Lev. 25:4) was ordained to bless His people with rest, peace, and prosperity, so the enemy set up the seven-year debt cycle to steal our peace and bring stress, confusion, and devastation.

Jim and I prayed and renounced those vows our ancestors had made, which had opened the door to that financial curse. We closed that door on behalf of ourselves, our children, and the generations to follow. Then we agreed with God, through the name and the blood of Jesus Christ, that the power of that spirit was broken over our lives. We appropriated and enforced the victory that Jesus won for us on the cross.

Next, we got our checkbooks and every financial document we could think of and put them in the center of our dining room table. Then we prayed over them and set them apart (consecrated them) to God. We gave Jesus lordship over our finances and called forth the blessings of God. The beautiful thing we realized was that even in the midst of what the enemy had tried to do to us, we had still experienced God's redemptive power to restore and to bless us with good things.

BREAKTHROUGH

By this time, we were already members of Gateway Church in Southlake, Texas. That was another significant marker in our financial journey, because the life message of our pastor, Robert Morris, is "the blessed life." We always knew that we would be blessed as we embraced his anointed teaching on this critical subject—and we have been.

Shortly after our warfare prayer and time of dedicating our finances to God, the Lord laid it on our hearts to give a large gift to our building campaign at church. Frankly, after all we had been through, it was scary. It was a big chunk of the savings we had left. Part of me was excited about giving to the work of God, but another part of me was hesitant. Taking into consideration that we knew God had spoken, I freely agreed with my husband to "do it afraid." I can still feel the queasiness in my stomach after we dropped the check into the offering box. Jim was at perfect peace, but I must admit, it took me a while.

In a few short months, we received back the amount we had given and it had multiplied ten times. Some would call that a tenfold return. Amazingly I didn't even think of it when we received the money. The morning after, when I awakened and opened my eyes, the Lord spoke to me that we had received a tenfold return on our gift. I hurried into the kitchen to tell Jim what the Lord told me. He was busily making breakfast as I shared with him. We laughed, became teary eyed, and then we thanked the Lord together. We both knew that we had finally broken through to the financial blessing God had always intended for us.

Until Jim's death in 2006, we enjoyed living the blessing. Provision flowed for our every need. The dark cloud that always seemed to hang over our family and finances was gone. I only wish Jim could have enjoyed it for a longer period of time before he died—but he's in heaven with the One who owns the cattle on a thousand hills (Ps. 50:10)! In my widowhood God continues to bless me. He's a great husband and provider!

Are you living in financial bondage? In our case it was caused by a demonic assignment against our family. If you've noticed a pattern of calamities that have been outside your realm of control, then this is a strong indicator that some kind of curse may be operating. Perhaps God is speaking to you about generational issues that require freedom. Or maybe He is drawing you to become faithful in giving or a more accountable money manager? Whatever the case, I encourage you to do the following activation and see what the Holy Spirit wants to reveal to you.

ACTIVATION EXERCISE

Get quiet before the Lord and let Him speak to you as you ask Him the following questions:

- Lord, is there an area related to finances where I am not experiencing the blessing? Is there an area of sin and iniquity that You want to identify in me or my family?

- What are the lie/lies that I/we have believed about finances? What is the truth according to Your Word?

Now repent and renounce any wrong beliefs, sins, or iniquities:

- ○ Cancel any generational bloodline curses or any spirit of death that is attacking your finances.

- ○ Declare that the power of the enemy has been broken in the name of Jesus and by the power of His blood that has redeemed you from the curse.

- ○ Open your heart to receive God's blessings by renewing your thinking with what He has promised you in His Word. For example, He calls you a coheir with Jesus, and He promises to bless you so that you will lend to others and not have to borrow. (See Deuteronomy 15:6 and 28:12–13; Ephesians 1:17–23 and 2:1–10; and 3 John 1:2.)

Use this sample prayer to get you started in this activation. Remember to be specific when you pray and declare the enemy's power broken. Open your heart to receive God's blessing.

God, I thank You for setting me free from any family hindrance to receiving financial blessings. Forgive me (and my family of origin) for any areas where I/we have disobeyed Your Word in regard to our finances. I break any curse (consequence of sin or wrong thinking), and I command any spirit to leave that has hindered blessing in my *life. (For example, poverty spirit, death in debt spirit, spirit of mammon*, or worldly spirit— name the spirit or describe its function.) I invite Jesus to be Lord over my finances. Amen.**

---

* Some Bible translations define *mammon* as money. However, it is more than that. Mammon is a wicked spirit that operates through money causing people to worship it as an idol. When people are under this spirit's control, they replace their dependence upon God with money and allow it to rule every aspect of their lives.

Chapter 7

SPIRITUAL GENETICS TRANSFER

Y OUR FAMILY DNA influences your life, but it is not your destiny. As Dr. Caroline Leaf wrote, "Genes do not cause behavior, they give us certain tendencies to behave in certain ways, but your genes do not have the final say...you do."[1] You are not your father. You are not your mother. You are not your ancestors. But the lives they led can help you determine:

- o The way you learned to think and process life

- o The ways you respond or react to events or circumstances

- o Habits you developed

- o Your life patterns (good and bad)

- o The way you see yourself, God, and others

- o Your struggles with various temptations

Learning about genetics and generational iniquity might make you think you have no control over your life. There can be a sense of being "doomed" if you had bad family genes, and that sometimes is used as an excuse for doing what you want to do—as if you have no power over your own behavior. This is completely untrue. Our genes do not have to control our emotions and behaviors, though they do factor into the equation.

We always have choices and must take responsibility for our actions, regardless of our DNA. Choices begin in your thought life, and thinking differently can turn the ship of your life around and point it in the direction you want to go. In order to live differently, you must think differently by renewing your mind to agree with God's Word. Negative, wrong thinking—whether it began with you or was passed down generationally—can become self-defeating and will prevent you from experiencing your dreams. Until you change those wrong thought patterns, you won't get the results you desire.

Fear and Worry—My DNA

I come from a long line of worriers. Worry has probably been the single most difficult thing in my life to overcome. I believe God showed me many years ago that it has been a part of the DNA on both the maternal and paternal sides of my family. It was a way of life that I observed growing up. Please understand that most of my family members are strong believers in Jesus Christ and wonderful individuals. But worrying was simply a way of life for them. If you didn't worry, you didn't care. That is the lie we believed.

Worry is the product of fear. I am persuaded that some of my ancestors opened the door to fear due to some traumatic events in their lives. Worry became one of the manifestations of the spirit of fear that dominated my family lineage. It's taken me a lifetime to get free, mostly because

I didn't understand for a long time the subtleties of how this generational bent toward worry had crippled me. Nor did I realize how deeply the demonic stronghold of fear had gripped every part of me. I take full responsibility for my responses to various life events. In each case I chose to align with worry and fear and gave it power. It's just that my generational bent made me really good at it! I spent a good deal of my life being ignorant of the enemy's devices, and I didn't recognize how his lies fed my fears.

Years ago, when we were attending The Church on the Way in California, Pastor Jack Hayford invited Rev. Dick Mills to minister there. He was prophetically gifted, and many people accepted Christ and some were also greatly encouraged when he "read their mail," so to speak. I was serving on staff at that time, and I will never forget when Dick Mills looked straight at me and said, "Young lady, God is going to deliver you from fear!" Then he had his wife read Psalm 91 over me. I was in shock! I thought, "Me? Have a spirit of fear?" I had no idea. Looking back, I should have known, because it really didn't take a rocket scientist to figure it out!

I was a grown woman in my thirties at the time, and I began a soul search like never before. I prayed continually for God to teach me about fear and help me recognize and understand how fear was paralyzing my life. One by one, memories began to surface of traumatic things that had happened to me growing up. Most of them had taken place when I was a baby.

God gave me a dream that I later shared with my mother. It was a dream about my dad when I was about six months old. In the dream, I was red in the face from crying and couldn't be comforted. I was obviously terrified. Daddy was putting a pillow over my face and moving it around in a playful way. To him, he was just playing with his baby daughter. But to me, that action produced the fear of being suffocated and the feeling of being powerless for the first time. An innocent (but rough) playtime began a lifetime of bondage for me.

My dad was an incredible man, and everyone loved him. He was fun, relational, and a successful businessman. You never felt judged by him. He occasionally dealt with anger, but for the most part only our family ever saw it. People couldn't imagine he would ever get mad, but he did. And I can remember walking on eggshells when I was a kid so I didn't upset him. In his later years he became much mellower, and I seldom saw him angry. That's probably why it was difficult to remember some of those events from my childhood, because he had changed so much. Let me be very clear: my father never hit me or abused me in any way other than emotionally, and even that wasn't intentional. He would have taken a bullet for me. Nevertheless, I reacted to his "playfulness" and occasional anger by being intimidated and fearful. I felt powerless. And those feelings shaped much of my life.

Over a period of time, the Holy Spirit led me to remember a number of instances that caused me to fear. I came to realize something very important: my perception of those events was as significant as the events themselves. Early on, my perceptions taught me to feel powerless, and this was coupled with the generational fear that already existed in the family. As I came into agreement with fear early on, it then became a way of life.

Behind every fear is a lie—and I believed lots of them. I believed I was controlled and powerless. It was not until

I was an adult that I was able to process all of this and let go of the fear that had bound me along with those feelings of powerlessness. It has been a long process, but I am continually learning to lean on Jesus and trust Him—because He has my back!

When you deal with generational iniquity, it is important to understand how the issues and struggles that marked previous generations can potentially flow down to you. In the remainder of this chapter, I will offer brief descriptions of four possible ways generational iniquity can be transmitted.

GENETIC TRANSMISSION

Generational iniquity can be transferred literally through your bloodline. This can manifest through physical conditions, personality traits, or behavioral tendencies.

Physical conditions

When we go to the doctor, physicians always ask what physical conditions existed in our families of origin. In fact, doctors require us to fill out long, tiresome forms to explain our family's medical history. This is because illnesses are frequently passed down in families. A few examples are heart disease, diabetes, arthritis, lupus, and cancer.

Personality traits

This includes our likes, dislikes, talents, weaknesses, and mannerisms. I heard about a study done in Israel that found facial expressions can be inherited. A woman was separated from her blind son for eighteen years, yet both had the same facial expressions. We all have stories about individuals in our families whose characteristics reflect those of another family member. We laugh at the similarities, but it demonstrates that certain tendencies are a part of our family DNA.

Behavioral tendencies

This has to do with a variety of things: the way we respond to situations, the way we like to eat, our sleeping habits and personal hygiene, the way we handle money, the priority we give to work, what we do for entertainment, and even the way we handle stress. It's true that some of these behaviors are learned through observation, but not always.

As I've said before, our DNA doesn't have to define us. Just because we have a family history of diabetes or high blood pressure, or generations of our ancestors have been workaholics, poor financial managers, or fearful, we don't have to follow the same path. We can break negative family patterns, even those passed down genetically.

Transmission by Example

We tend to repeat what we have seen lived out before us. You've heard the saying, "Monkey see, monkey do!" Here's a visual example of that. I heard a story once about a female dog that was expected to deliver her puppies very soon. Somehow she got in front of her master's lawn mower and both of her hind legs were cut off. She was taken to a vet and then medicated, bandaged, and given some serious TLC by her owners. The vet assured them that she would recover and deliver the pups just fine.

Once the dog's healing process began, she taught herself to get around by moving her hind end from side to side until she reached her destination. Can you get a visual of that? I certainly can! She learned to maneuver just fine, and just as the vet had predicted, she delivered her puppies in a few weeks. After a time of nursing and caring for her pups, they began to walk. You probably already guessed it—they walked just like her!

We all have adopted some behaviors that were transmitted by example. Children are especially vulnerable to this process. They imitate what they see their parents live out before them. God designed families to create a positive environment where each new generation can learn to survive and thrive. However, He never intended for parents to train the next generation without His help. Unfortunately when ancestors don't follow the Lord's ways, it sets a negative example that produces generational iniquity. The children of Israel did this again and again.

One example is found in the Book of Jeremiah:

> The LORD said, "It is because they have forsaken my
> law, which I set before them; they have not obeyed
> me or followed my law. Instead, they have followed
> the stubbornness of their hearts; they have followed
> the Baals, as their ancestors taught them."
>   —JEREMIAH 9:13–14

This is contrary to the positive legacy of generational blessing God had intended:

> Only be careful, and watch yourselves closely so that
> you do not forget the things your eyes have seen or
> let them fade from your heart as long as you live.
> Teach them to your children and to their children
> after them. Remember the day you stood before

the LORD your God at Horeb, when he said to me, "Assemble the people before me to hear my words so that they may learn to revere me as long as they live in the land and may teach them to their children."

—DEUTERONOMY 4:9–10

Fix these words of mine in your hearts and minds; tie them as symbols on your hands and bind them on your foreheads. Teach them to your children, talking about them when you sit at home and when you walk along the road, when you lie down and when you get up. Write them on the doorframes of your houses and on your gates, so that your days and the days of your children may be many in the land the LORD swore to give your ancestors, as many as the days that the heavens are above the earth.

—DEUTERONOMY 11:18–21

God wants us to transmit by example His blessings to future generations instead of transmitting the curse of generational iniquity. We must break these negative generational patterns by appropriating the finished work of Christ. Scripture says, He "has redeemed us from the curse of the Law, having become a curse for us" (Gal. 3:13, NAS).

TRANSMISSION THROUGH THE LAW OF SOWING AND REAPING

God originally established the law of sowing and reaping for the purpose of blessing. When Adam and Eve sinned, the curse came into the earth. Therefore, the law that was intended for blessing became an avenue for destruction as well. Galatians 6:7–8 tells us:

Do not be deceived, God is not mocked; for whatever a man sows, that he will also reap. For he who sows to his flesh will of the flesh reap corruption but he who sows to the Spirit will of the Spirit reap everlasting life.

—NKJV

My grandparents were West Texas cotton farmers who knew the principles of sowing and reaping. They understood that you can only harvest what you plant. If you plant green beans, you don't get squash! You can't plant a peach tree and get plums. Whatever you sow into the ground is what you get in return.

It's the same with life. We make choices and decisions that determine our future, and they profoundly affect generations to come. We cannot sow bad seed and expect to reap all the blessings God has planned for us in this life. Therefore, it is important to consider the following aspects of sowing and reaping:

You usually reap what you sow (apart from God's mercy)

You have plowed wickedness. You have reaped iniquity.

—Hosea 10:13, MEV

You usually reap more than you sow
Sowing evil produces multiplied effects:

For they sow the wind, and they will reap the whirlwind.

—Hosea 8:7, MEV

But sowing good seed in good ground reaps multiplied blessing:

> Others, like seed sown on good soil, hear the word, accept it, and produce a crop—some thirty, some sixty, some a hundred times what was sown.
> —MARK 4:20

You usually reap later than you sow

> And let us not grow weary in doing good, for in due season we shall reap, if we do not give up.
> —GALATIANS 6:9, MEV

> Some men's sins are evident, pointing to judgment, but other men's sins are revealed later. Likewise, the good works of some are evident, but those that are not cannot be hidden.
> —1 TIMOTHY 5:24–25, MEV

If you are reaping bad seed that was sown in your generation or previous generations, repent, renounce, and break the enemy's power. Begin a new legacy as you sow good seed that will result in blessings.

TRANSMISSION THROUGH DEMONIC OPPRESSION

Demons can be transferred down the family line through an ancestral or generational curse. Some examples of this are family bloodlines that have been dedicated to false gods through satanic rituals or Masonic curses. Demons that stay within families are often referred to as "familiar spirits." Demons can also transfer from one person to another through soul ties. Soul ties are often formed when strong emotional bonds are created, such as through sexual union. (See Proverbs 7:24–27 and 1 Corinthians 6:16, 18.) In his later years Solomon went astray into idolatry and worshipped false gods (demonic spirits) because of the influence of his many pagan wives (1 Kings 11:1–10).

Whenever curses (consequences) exist or a person has opened doors to the enemy, those doors must be closed and that demonic bondage destroyed in order for that individual to walk in freedom. We serve a powerful God who is fully able to give us understanding and guide us through the process of freedom so we can experience His original design for our lives. And He has given us authority over demons and all the power of the enemy through the name of Jesus (Luke 10:17–20).

To sum up what we've discussed in this chapter, it is not genetics that determines the quality of our lives. The choices we make today will determine our future. God said in His Word:

> Now listen! Today I am giving you a choice between life and death, between prosperity and disaster.
> —DEUTERONOMY 30:15, NLT

> This day I call the heavens and the earth as witnesses against you that I have set before you life and death, blessings and curses. Now choose life, so that you and your children may live and that you may love the LORD your God, listen to his voice, and hold fast to him.
> —DEUTERONOMY 30:19–20

We may have to contend with negative traits from our families of origin, but we never lose our ability to choose.

ACTIVATION EXERCISE

As you have done previously, get quiet before the Lord and ask Him:

- o What are You saying to me through this chapter?

- o What choices have I made in the past that have produced the results I am experiencing today?

Listen for what He reveals to you. Then repent, renounce, and break your agreement with any generational iniquity. That means you must choose to think differently, turn your back on sin and darkness, and exercise your authority through the name of Jesus to break the power of the enemy over your life, according to Luke 10:19.

After you have done the above, ask the Lord to give you a glimpse of how your future will look differently as you leave the old lifestyle and patterns of behavior behind. Let the following prayer get you started in this activation:

> *Father, I declare that it is for freedom that You have set me free (Gal. 5:1). I choose now to live in freedom, not in bondage to the traits of my ancestors. I repent of the choices I've made that have empowered negative, ungodly traits to operate in my life. I renounce my allegiance to them (name the ungodly trait), and I break my agreement with their lies. I choose to abide in the truth of Your Word and live in the liberty You purchased for me on the cross.*

I ask now that You give me a glimpse of how different my future will look as I leave the old lifestyle and patterns of behavior behind. I desire all that You have for me and my family. In Jesus's name, amen.

Chapter 8

IN SEARCH OF A FATHER

A FEW YEARS AGO, I had the privilege of hearing the personal story of a remarkably successful Christian who had become a grown man before finally meeting his father. Yuri Star is a living example of how our personality genetics are transmitted from generation to generation. Several years ago, I invited Yuri to share his story during my teaching segment on generational iniquity at one of our KAIROS freedom events at Gateway Church. We all sat stunned as we heard how his search to find the father he had never met—and knew so little about—culminated in some life-defining discoveries. Recently I sat down with Yuri, who retold his remarkable story to me so that I could share it with you.

YURI'S BEGINNINGS

The history of Yuri's family plays like an early 1970s movie. His mom and dad were two hippies who got together during a road trip. Yuri was conceived not long after they met, and the two parted ways long before Yuri's mother knew she was pregnant.

After learning she was expecting, his mother decided to come up with a completely new name for her baby. One night, inspired by the stars shining down on the beach, she came up with the name Yuri Lite Star. After moving to California, she gave birth to Yuri. Later she explained to him that she had received somewhat of a vision regarding his birth—that he would be the first of a new lineage.

He was the only Star in his family. His mother had three sons from her previous marriage, so Yuri had three older half-brothers—all with more traditional names. He always felt like the odd man out because he was so different from his brothers. Yuri and his family led a "super free" hippie lifestyle—if you want to call it truly "free"! Sadly, little Yuri was smoking marijuana by the time he was eight years old. Then he sold pot to support himself when he moved out of the house at age twelve.

At seventeen, Yuri met a pastor who preached about the love and grace of God, and Yuri came to know Christ. Eventually, he was encouraged to leave his surfer-hippie lifestyle in Hawaii to get an education on the mainland. He moved to Dallas, Texas, where he attended Christ for the Nations Institute (CFNI). One day, Yuri was listening to Carol Thompson, an outstanding teacher at CFNI, talk about father wounds. He was intrigued. By this time, Yuri was about twenty-five years old, and he was beginning to recognize that he had some identity issues.

Yuri had always thought he was fine with never knowing his dad. After all, he had always been very independent. In his way of viewing things, he had made it very well on his own without a father and really didn't need to unearth or rehash the past. Now, for the first time in his life, he was beginning to wonder if maybe he should find out more about his biological father.

Yuri's Search for His Father

After recognizing that it would be beneficial to meet his dad, Yuri inquired of his mom about his dad's whereabouts, trying to get all the information from her that he could. Afterward, he did an Internet search and found sixty leads. His very first phone call was a match—he had located his father! A young man named Bobby answered the phone, and Yuri soon discovered that Bobby was his younger half-brother. Yuri asked him a number of questions to make sure he had the right house. He quizzed him about their grandparents and asked about family members residing in central California. He asked Bobby if his dad worked in television. His brother just answered, "Yes." Then Yuri asked if his dad was home, and Bobby said, "Not at this time."

It took Yuri months to work up the nerve to call his father again. This time his dad answered the phone and introduced himself. Then he said, "I was wondering when you would call." He went on to say, "I want you to know that I am a responsible man, and I didn't know that your mother wasn't on birth control."

"Secondly," he said, "I'm glad you called, because there are some genetics in the family that you need to be aware of." His father's random responses caused Yuri to begin to connect some dots. When he got to this part of the story, Yuri told me, "Linda, those would have been my responses if I had done the same thing he had done. I would have been the responsible one."

Yuri explained to his father, "There are two reasons I'm calling. First, I want to let you know that I am alive. Second, I am engaged to be married." At the time of this conversation, Yuri had just gotten a promotion on his job, and one of his assignments was to fly to California four to six times a year. Would you believe that the office he visited was located within fifteen minutes of his dad's work?

YURI MEETS HIS DAD

Over the following year, Yuri finally got to know his father. When he made his first trip to California, he was scheduled to meet his dad. They arranged to connect at the Sony Building in San Jose. Yuri stood outside, anxiously watching as a sea of people entered and exited the building. How in the world would he recognize his father when he had no earthly idea what he looked like? All of a sudden, a blond-headed, blue-eyed man stepped out of the elevator (Yuri has dark hair). "I knew it was him," Yuri said to me, with a great big grin on his face, as if he were experiencing it all over again. "The moment he stepped out of the elevator I knew it had to be him because my dad is Norwegian and my mom is Hispanic. I just knew," he said.

As Yuri talked with his father, he discovered that they were in exactly the same line of work: media and computers. They both had an intense passion for music and loved to play the guitar. Yuri was amazed to find out they even loved the same particular kind of jazz and collected albums and CDs from the same artists. Although his dad had absolutely no input into Yuri's life (other than through his bloodline), they were amazingly similar in personality, likes and dislikes, talents, and mannerisms—even though they'd never met!

Yuri married his wife, Marissa, in 1998, and they made their home in the Dallas area. In 2002 Yuri's dad called when he was visiting Dallas on business. It was just after the birth of Yuri and Marissa's first son, Caleb. Marissa wanted a picture of the three of them. As the photo was being taken, Yuri's father said, "Wow! Amazing! Three generations!"

"When he acknowledged the three generations, he became Grandpa," Yuri told me, grinning from ear to ear. Yuri and Marissa now have four sons. His family is the first generation of "Stars," and Yuri believes God gave him a spiritual reset, beginning with that unique name his mother chose for him.

An interesting side note: when Marissa and Yuri first met and became engaged, she told him that as a teenager she had often written her name as "Marissa Star" on her junior high school notebooks. When Yuri didn't believe her, she took him to her room and pulled out those old notebooks to prove it to him. There it was plain as day: "Marissa Star" scribbled on her notebooks.

Indeed, their story is an incredible one with the redemptive hand of God laced all through their experiences. Both Yuri and Marissa brought lots of baggage into their marriage and family. Marissa had been a meth addict and came from a broken family. She and Yuri will be the first to tell you regarding marriage and parenting, "We are still figuring it out." Having watched them from a distance for a number of years, I can honestly say they are doing a great job. I love their hearts and their commitment to serve Christ and allow Him to change them whenever necessary.

In 2006 Yuri founded his own company, Church Media Group, based in Keller, Texas. Marissa is the founder and former executive director of *Destiny in Bloom*, an online devotional that reaches twenty thousand to thirty thousand people per month. She is still a contributing writer to the blog. They are truly a couple who mirror Christ's powerful work of restoration, and God uses them in profound ways to impact and encourage others.

ICING ON THE CAKE

Yuri's story becomes more astonishing each time I hear it. We all love a happy ending, but that's not the only thing that draws me back to hear it again and again. I am touched with the manner in which Yuri was able to embrace life and move forward, regardless of whether he had a father in his life or not. He sought after spiritual fathers to receive the fathering he never had.

Here is an illustration of what I mean. Yuri was an executive pastor of media at Gateway Church in Southlake, Texas. When he transitioned from the church into his own business in 2006, he served as a great model for leaving a job and church well. He asked for the blessing of leadership (those who had fathered and mentored him) before making a move. He received a blessing along with the assurance that whether he succeeded or failed, they were for him!

Most importantly Yuri embraced his heavenly Father and allowed Him to nurture and mentor his heart. As a result, Yuri had forgiven his earthly father before they ever met. So being united with his dad was the icing on the cake but not the cake itself. Our relationship with God must always be our most important focus, then every-thing else becomes the icing on the cake. This is how our lives become impeccably balanced, healthy, and whole.

FATHERS IMPART TO THEIR CHILDREN

Fathers are intended to be gifts from God. However, the word *father* incites different responses depending upon a person's experience. For some it brings a picture of love, tenderness, laughter, safety, and authority. For others it may bring images of rejection, neglect, abuse, fear, disap-pointment, and failure.

God is our model of fatherhood. He leads and influ-ences with perfect love. He considers the role of fathers to be a top priority. But many modern societies have lowered the standard of fathering and in some cases have reduced it to a biological paternity test.

In contrast, God's idea of true fatherhood has to do with impartation. Fathers should impart identity and des-tiny to their children. The Apostle Paul wrote:

> Fathers, do not provoke your children to anger by the way you treat them. Rather, bring them up with the discipline and instruction that comes from the Lord.
> —EPHESIANS 6:4, NLT

If we're really honest, we all have a deep longing to be loved by a father. Some of us were fortunate enough to have that privilege, and others were not. We can all attest to the fact that we long to be held by a father and receive a personal, meaningful connection with him. We yearn to have affirming words spoken to us by a father and to be secure in the knowledge that we are valued and loved. How many people feel they had no clear objective for their life because they had no father speak encouragement and direction concerning their future?

The Bible shows us examples of Jewish children being blessed. Their lives were actually prophesied over and declarations were made concerning who they would become. In the Old Testament, we read the words Isaac spoke to Jacob:

> Therefore, may God give you of the dew of heaven and the fatness of the earth, and plenty of grain and new wine. Let peoples serve you, and nations bow down to you. Be master over your brothers, and let your mother's sons bow down to you. Cursed be everyone who curses you, and blessed be those who bless you!
>
> —GENESIS 27:28–29, MEV

None of these things were true at the time that Isaac spoke these words to Jacob. Isaac was calling forth what was to be, as God prophetically spoke through him. The father's blessing was practiced faithfully in the Jewish culture. Today, at the very least, we should instill hope in our children's hearts for their future by declaring the strengths and God-given gifts we see in them, and by giving them meaningful goals with helpful direction for their future. How incredible it would be for fathers to seek the heart of God regarding their children and then call those things forth in their lives.

We live in a fatherless generation where it's not uncommon for a son or daughter to have an orphaned heart, even with the father living right there in the household. Many don't know where their fathers are or even who they are. The Apostle Paul understood this travesty and the need for fathering when he proclaimed to the Corinthians that they had many teachers among them but not many fathers (1 Cor. 4:15). Paul recognized the importance of having a true father who would take the time and effort to help his children grow up well.

In the absence of an earthly father, it is so good to know we have a heavenly Father who said He would be a father to the fatherless (Ps. 68:5)! He is continually proclaiming who we are and imparting identity where none has been given from an earthly father. Let's face it: the best of fathers are imperfect. So aren't we grateful to be loved and cared for by our perfect heavenly Father? He will make up the difference, regardless of our story. And He will redeem what has been lost—just as He did with Yuri Lite Star.

One of the greatest reasons individuals find themselves stuck and unable to advance is because of father (or mother) wounds. God wants to restore our orphaned or abandoned hearts so we can know Him and receive healing in those wounded places. Some of us have learned to be fathered by God in those areas where our own dads didn't know how to be effective fathers, or perhaps simply neglected to fulfill their God-given assignment to father their children.

You are mightily loved by your heavenly Father. Open your heart to believe and receive His perfect love that removes all fear!

ACTIVATION EXERCISE

Before doing the activation below, meditate upon 1 John 4:15–16 and 2 Timothy 1:7. As we've done in previous chapters, find a private place, quiet your heart, and ask your heavenly Father the following questions. Listen for His answers. You will be astounded and amazed!

- o Father, is there an area of my heart that You want to father?

- o What do You want to be to me right now that I have never allowed You to be?

- o Father, would You give me a visual of what You want our relationship to look like?

- o Father, please heal all the wounds, hurts, disappointments, and scars of the past where my father was less than what a father should be. Change my thinking where there are misconceptions about who You really are as a result of who my earthly father was or is. Help me identify the lies that I have believed and replace them with Your truth.

- o I choose to forgive my dad, just as You forgave those who hurt You. (Now speak out the specific things your earthly father did that you need to forgive. Acknowledge the emotions you felt when those things happened, and ask God to exchange the negative emotions with positive ones. For example, replace fear with love, unrest with peace, and rejection with acceptance.)

Remember to grant forgiveness for the wrong or hurtful things he did, and also for the things you feel deep in your heart that you needed but your dad neglected to give you (love, direction, affection, guidance, affirmation, quality time, etc.).

o Make this declaration: "I release my earthly father from any judgments (name those judgments) that I have made against him (let it go), and I bless him in Jesus's name."

Now I encourage you to pray the following:

Heavenly Father, I thank You that You are the perfect Father and that You love me unconditionally. Help me to receive Your love and to know that I am Your son (daughter). I long to be fathered by You and to understand my true identity in Christ. In Your name, amen.

Chapter 9

TYPE O + TYPE O = TYPE O SO WHY AM I TYPE A?

H AVE YOU EVER watched (and gotten hooked on) the television series *The Locator*? Just in case you are unfamiliar with this cable network show, it is a tearjerker! As I faithfully watched each week, I made sure my Kleenex box was next to my chair in preparation for my emotional responses to family reunions.

Troy Dunn, executive producer and star of the short-lived television show, reunites people with long-lost loved ones. Those who want to find a family member contact Troy to discover their whereabouts. He uses every tool and piece of software available to find the individual's location. Then he summons his jet and creates an emotional meeting that will stir your heart.

Dana Sellar's story may not be quite as dramatic as some on *The Locator,* yet in some ways hers is even more moving! God Himself led her, in a most unusual way, to connect the dots generationally and genetically to her early beginnings. He assisted her in receiving healing from the roots of early childhood rejection. I think you will be fascinated by the story of her long-awaited reunion.

DANA'S STORY

Dana struggled with rejection her whole life. When she attended one of our KAIROS freedom events at Gateway Church, she dealt with a major portion of it. Yet something still remained. She continued to struggle with feelings of being "left out" and "not fitting in." Dana blew it off many times, thinking she just needed to get over it, put on her "big girl panties," and suck it up! Deep down she knew there was a root of rejection she had not yet discovered.

In 2009 Dana's brother Eric died of a drug overdose. Dana and Eric were very close, so after his death there was a huge void in her heart. She didn't know how to *not* be a sister to Eric. She began to spin out of control. Questions regarding her birth began to surface in her heart, as they often did when she was growing up. Dana looked nothing like her father or her siblings, and her personality and mannerisms were opposite too! To top it off, she was left-handed while they were all right-handed. She thought, "What if my father is not my real father, and I have another brother or sister out there someplace?"

Her parents, Freddie and Lana, got married when he was sixteen and she was nineteen. Both came from very dysfunctional families. Marriage seemed like the best way to flee their neglectful and chaotic home lives. They each had often been left to themselves while growing up, and they sought love and acceptance in each other.

A baby boy was born during their first year of marriage, and marital problems soon followed. They decided not to divorce but to begin dating other people. In their worldly mind-sets, that made perfect sense to them in that season of their lives. Lana started dating a guy I'll call Johnny and soon became pregnant with her daughter, Dana.

When she went to Johnny to tell him about her pregnancy, Lana was floored when he told her that his wife was pregnant also! Lana, feeling sure that Dana was Freddie's baby anyway, went back to Freddie, and they reconciled for the sake of the child. When Dana was about a year old, problems began to surface again in their marriage and this time they divorced.

Lana found Christ and became radically changed from the darkness of living life in clubs. Shortly afterward, Freddie also received Christ as his Savior. Their lives both changed drastically, and Freddie and Lana remarried when Dana was four years old.

Dana had questioned off and on most of her life if Freddie was truly her biological father. People would ask her, "Why are you so tall and most of your family is not?" Dana ran track, and she can still remember people asking her where she got her speed. Different ones would ask random questions that caused her to wonder. And she just had a gut feeling. Although Freddie was a wonderful father and she couldn't ask for anything more from a dad, Dana couldn't help but feel that he might not be her biological dad.

SEARCHING FOR TRUTH

Soon after Eric's death in 2009, Dana decided to get in touch with an aunt who knew about her parents' past. She had to have answers. Dana spent the night with her aunt and the questioning began. She asked about when she was conceived and the timing of her birth. The aunt carefully answered her questions and also told her the doctor and others had suggested her mother get an abortion.

Dana, married at that point, returned home from her aunt's house and began to talk with her husband. "I'm bothered by all of this," she told him. "Before, I didn't need to know, but since Eric's death, I do. I may have another sibling out there someplace!" It was clear Dana had more questions that needed answers, and her husband, Scott, encouraged her to continue her search and find out more information.

The next day, Dana told her best friend about the information she had gleaned from her aunt, including the counsel her mother had received to abort Dana. Her friend's instant reply was, "There's your root of rejection." Dana had a vision of a tree being ripped out of the ground when she prayed for God to heal her heart. The Holy Spirit showed Dana that it was a root of rejection from conception that was being healed.

Dana attended KAIROS for a second time fairly soon after her visit with her aunt. She received still more healing from rejection. Just as important, she received encouragement. A woman at the conference had a prophetic word from God for her: "God has called you for a very specific purpose. Your time is now. You are a force to be reckoned with. You tick the enemy off when you wake up. You have felt like something is wrong with you. God was not waiting on you to 'act better' or 'do more.' He was waiting for you to be healed of a deep wound." She was right—it was the wound of rejection.

Dana was now in hard pursuit of truth. She considered DNA tests and discussed it with her siblings. She saw pictures of Johnny that her mother had saved. He was tall and had dark hair. His full name was on the back of one of the photos, so she now had enough information to begin googling his name to gain insights into his life. But for some reason she still didn't have a peace about proceeding with DNA tests.

A SURPRISING DISCLOSURE

In the midst of her search, Freddie—the father who had raised her—was diagnosed with non-Hodgkin's lymphoma. Dana's search for truth was put on hold so she could focus on getting her dad healthy. One evening, as they visited in the living room of her parents' house, she and Freddie were discussing blood types. Her dad mentioned that he was a type O, and her mom said, "Oh, me too!" Dana had been doing her homework, so she knew the answer to her long-awaited question: O + O = O. Dana was a type A.

Dana kept quiet and didn't share her secret with her parents. At a later time, she spoke to her mother, who had realized the same thing the night of their conversation, though she had remained silent about it. She was brokenhearted for Dana and asked her to forgive her. Dana assured her mom that she was forgiven—completely!

Dana also told her dad about her blood type in case he hadn't realized he was not her biological father. He had not. Freddie had an amazing response: "You are my girl. You are my girl! That is not going to change. Are you OK? How are you?" Dana asked him if he was OK and he said, "Yes, I'm OK. This doesn't change anything. You are my girl and your kids are my grandbabies." His first response was concern for Dana, not for himself. Dana can't tell this part of the story without crying. The restorative work of God is unparalleled. The Lord later told Dana, "Freddie is your daddy. You two share the same blood with Me—the only blood that matters." That brought absolute peace to her heart.

During all the family research, Dana discovered that she had a younger brother and an older sister whom Johnny had fathered. And they both attended her church! She and her sister made a date to go to Starbucks to get to know each other. During this meeting, it was revealed that Johnny was left-handed just like Dana. They both are tall and thin with dark hair and dark skin. Like Dana, Johnny loved to run track and was a very fast sprinter. When she saw his younger pictures, they looked so much alike!

Johnny and Dana tend to be the life of the party at gatherings, while Freddie is laid back and quiet. They have the same personality—one that walks into a room and takes charge! Dana said to me in the interview, "Johnny is my choleric personality but untamed and unredeemed! God knew it would be better for me, spiritually, if Freddie raised me."

Happy Endings

God helped Dana unravel her story, and He did it without disrupting or unsettling her family life or the lives of her extended family. Johnny's entire family welcomed Dana with open arms—even Johnny's wife. They believe Dana adds something to the family that was missing. Johnny doesn't always know what to do with her because she is so much like him. She can say things to him that the rest of the family can't get away with at all!

Thanks to Freddie's suggestion, Johnny now enjoys spending time with Dana and Scott's four children. Freddie told Dana, "If I had four grandchildren out there, I would want to know them."

Dana's search for where her root of rejection began took her back before her own birth. And the root of rejection her parents carried (because of the way they had been neglected growing up) most likely could be traced to their parents, grandparents, or even further back as well. This is how "familiar" (family) spirits operate. The cycle of pain and dysfunction will be perpetuated until someone breaks it through the power and grace of God.

Dana is beginning a new legacy in her family as she embraces the acceptance and love that only our heavenly Father can provide. And that legacy is free of rejection! With new confidence she can now face her future and embrace the plans and purposes of God for her life. And, just as importantly, she and Scott will instill that in their four precious children so they can pass it on to their children…and their children's children.

There are many more parts to this story that are interesting and worth recording. I am urging Dana to put it into a book of her own. It is her story to tell, and I so appreciate her allowing me to share some of it with you. Her family provides a great picture of God healing a generational root of rejection.

I love hearing each person's journey of healing. It's so amazing how no two are ever alike. Our loving Father is nothing short of amazing! His pathway to healing and freedom is unique for each of us.

Overcoming Rejection

One can't help but be moved at the way Dana resolved to get to the bottom of her feelings of rejection. She pursued her freedom with all of her heart, even though that took her down some trails where she didn't expect to go. That happens sometimes as we pursue getting to the root of issues that are frustrating and defeating—but the difficult journey is well worth it! As Earl G. Graves once said, "We keep going back, stronger, not weaker, because we will not allow rejection to beat us down. It will only strengthen our resolve. To be successful there is no other way."[1]

Rejection is denial of love. When we feel rejected, we feel disapproval. When we are loved, we feel approval and acceptance. The experience of rejection shapes our core beliefs and sense of identity. As a result, we develop defense mechanisms to protect ourselves instead of allowing God to protect us. If you are suffering from a root of rejection, see if you recognize any of the following defense mechanisms in yourself:

- o Rebellion
- o Perfectionism
- o False responsibility
- o Material lust
- o Sexual attention-getting methods
- o Self-promotion
- o Controlling others
- o Bitterness

- ○ Escapism

- ○ Defensiveness

- ○ Guilt

- ○ Hopelessness

Considering that most everyone has experienced rejection at some level, it only makes sense to devote this chapter's activation to that subject. Allow the Holy Spirit to direct you to any roots of rejection you might be experiencing. Ask Him to pinpoint any source of rejection, whether it came through an experience you had, through your generational bloodlines, or maybe even rejection in the womb (as a result of an unwanted pregnancy or possibly an attempted abortion). Lastly, allow the Lord to heal those wounds and replace the feeling of rejection with His tender love and unconditional acceptance. The Lord says, "I have chosen [accepted] you and not rejected you" (Isa. 41:9, NAS).

ACTIVATION EXERCISE

As always, get quiet before the Lord and allow Him to speak to you as you seek Him through the following questions:

- ○ Holy Spirit, would You show me when I first experienced rejection? In the womb? A specific event? Is rejection an issue in my family of origin?

- ○ When did I come into agreement with rejection and believe the enemy's lies?

- ○ Lord, what is the truth?

- ○ Do I need to forgive anyone or release judgments?

- ○ Lord, heal my heart as I sit in Your presence and open my heart to receive Your acceptance.

When you've spent some time working through those questions, close your time with prayer.

Father, I thank You that You have not rejected me but You have chosen me. It is Your desire for me to love and be loved. I ask You to fill me anew with Your Holy Spirit and love for others. Heal the wounds of past rejection as I choose to forgive and let it go. I break the spirit of rejection and its power over me and my family in Jesus's name! Amen

It is vital that when you receive freedom you learn to maintain it. I discuss this further at the close of this book, but for now I encourage you to allow God to speak to you through His Word. Don't allow the enemy to steal the truth when hard times come. (See the Parable of the Sower in Matthew 13:1–9.) Study in particular those areas where you have known struggles. For example, if you struggle with rejection, look up all the scriptures on the subject of rejection and acceptance, and use the activation provided as often as needed, since it specifically addresses the subject of rejection.

Chapter 10

SINS OF THE FATHERS

'M GOING TO begin this chapter with a funny story to help us lighten up a bit.

As a man sat down in his seat on the fifty-yard line for the Super Bowl, a woman came along and asked him if anyone was sitting in the seat next to him. "No," he said, "the seat is empty."

The woman replied, "This is incredible! Who in their right mind would have a great seat like this for the Super Bowl—one of the biggest sporting events in the world—and not use it?"

Somberly the man answered, "Well...the seat was for my wife—since she and I had planned to come here together—but she passed away. This is the first Super Bowl we haven't been to together since we got married in '68."

The woman responded, "Oh, I'm sorry to hear that. That's terrible! But couldn't you find someone else—a friend or relative, or even a neighbor to take the seat?"

The man shook his head, "No, they are all at the funeral."

I find that story funny today. However, if I had heard it a number of years ago, I wouldn't have found it funny at all! Although my husband would have never sunk so low, he wasn't too far off. He was so hooked on sports that it could have cost him his family. It definitely cost him some of the love and adoration from his girls that he would have received had he been more balanced in his love for sports. Let me share some of our story with you.

THE DAY WAR BROKE OUT

What began as a beautiful Thanksgiving Day in Valencia, California, quickly turned into a war zone at the Godsey home. I had just completed cooking a wonderful feast when my husband announced (insisted) on watching football during our Thanksgiving dinner. When we all sat down to eat, we could hardly hear our Thanksgiving prayer for the noise of the football game blaring on the TV in the background. After numerous verbal warnings, I finally lost it—though that was no excuse for what followed! I can still remember the anger I felt as the blood rushed to my head and my hands pounded on the table. I insisted, "No football during Thanksgiving dinner!" I was furious, and my husband became more agitated by the moment, resulting in an exchange of words between us that wasn't pretty.

That occasion was one of the few times in our marriage when we argued in front of our children. And it caused me to make an appointment for counseling. I met with our pastor, Jack Hayford, to get some advice on what to do. I hoped he could help me make sense of what had happened on Thanksgiving and why that kind of conflict kept occurring. After exchanging a few pleasantries and hearing my story, Pastor Jack (as we called him) deduced that the enemy had inflicted a deep wound of rejection in my heart—and he did it using an old weapon from my past. Sports represented rejection from my father. You see, he was obsessed with it also, at least from my perspective. And now I was married to a man with the same obsession, and I felt rejected by him too. Are you connecting the dots yet?

HEALING ON SUPER BOWL SUNDAY

Many years ago when I arranged that meeting with our pastor, I had just begun my journey of freedom. In those days, The Church on the Way in Los Angeles was smaller, so Pastor Jack had more time for individual ministry. My husband and I were fairly new to the church; therefore, Pastor Jack knew very little about us. However, we had been there long enough to make a few friends.

My purpose for making the appointment was to talk about father wounds. God had clearly prompted me to talk with Pastor Jack, yet I had resisted for weeks because I was afraid of opening a can of worms. Frankly I also feared that he wouldn't have time (or make time) to see me. That's how people with father wounds feel! A wise counselor once told me, "If you see through the eyes of rejection, you're going to find it!" This is so true—you'll see rejection in everything.

I arrived that Sunday morning and my meeting with Pastor Jack began. As we talked, it was evident that most of my father wounds occurred during my childhood and early teen years. They revolved around the rejection I felt due to my father's love for sports. In my elementary and junior high years, my father was very involved in playing baseball himself, and he coached Pony League baseball teams, which was a league for older teenage boys. My dad almost always led his teams to win championships, and the players adored him! I loved and admired my daddy, and I found myself wanting to be one of those boys to whom he gave so much of his time. I knew Daddy was glad he had girls (my sister, Darlene, and me) because he often said so. But for whatever reason, it just didn't sink in how much he loved us.

My dad watched every sport on TV incessantly. He would promise to take us places on the weekend or play with us, but then it never happened. He probably didn't realize it, but he routinely broke promises to our family because he was so reluctant to miss one of those televised games. Pure and simple, he enjoyed his sports!

In his defense Dad worked hard when we were growing up. Sometimes he had a night job after working all day. He worked hard to provide for us. I knew deep down that my daddy loved me and would take a bullet for me. At this stage of my life, I can certainly understand his need to have down time, rest, and just "chill out!" But as a child I didn't understand that at all. My perception was that there was something wrong with *me*. "My daddy wishes I had been a boy," I thought. "I'm not important to him." This was my heart judgment concerning his choices. The enemy was busy working to magnify the rejection in my heart.

MONKEY SEE, MONKEY DO!

Did I mention that my dad's father always broke promises to him and his siblings? When I was growing up, my dad often told the story of how his father promised him a quarter to go to the movies. Can you even imagine getting into a movie for a quarter? Dad was just a small boy when it happened, but he remembered eagerly getting ready to go to the Saturday morning movie. As he headed out the door, he reached out his little hand for his movie money. His father then announced to him that he had changed his mind—for no apparent reason. Perhaps he didn't have any money; but he gave no explanation to his little boy.

As a grown man, my father told that story as if it happened yesterday. Evidently that sort of thing happened often. The incident made a lasting impression on my dad. He always had a hard time trusting people—especially authority figures. It makes perfect sense. I'm sure my grandfather didn't have evil intentions, but his actions became a snare for my dad. If you can't trust your own father to keep his word, why would you trust someone you hardly know?

The way my father related to me was (unconsciously) learned behavior from his father. Once again we see how behaviors are passed down through families. "Monkey see, monkey do!" Heart attitudes and priorities are transmitted to the succeeding generation.

My heart had become so hardened toward people who didn't keep their word that I made an inner vow: "I will never break promises to my children." And to my knowledge I never did. However, I later renounced that vow and put God into the driver's seat of my heart. I now say something like this: "By God's grace, I will keep my promises and never break my word to my children and grandchildren."

Daddy's failure to keep his promises also affected my ability to believe the promises of my heavenly Father. I later came to realize that we tend to relate to our heavenly Father in the same way we relate to our earthly dads—consciously or unconsciously. Even though our perfect heavenly Father never leaves, forsakes, or breaks His promises, we can subconsciously think of Him as having the same flaws and characteristics as our earthly father. Until our father wounds are forgiven and healed, it's difficult to trust, feel, and experience the love of God. We may know intellectually that He loves us, but we won't trust our heart to Him. One of the great truths about God is that He always keeps His promises to His children and He cannot lie (Titus 1:2).

FORGIVENESS GRANTED

Although I didn't realize it at the time, the appointment with Pastor Jack was about understanding the need to forgive my dad for being an "over the top" sports enthusiast at his family's expense. Because of the way I had perceived him, I needed to forgive him for breaking promises to me because of his love and preference for sports. I also had to address my need to release judgments against him so I could come to know and believe the love of my heavenly Father, who is always there for me. Unfortunately all the things my dad did right—and there were many—didn't enter into my mind at the time. It's amazing how the enemy uses the negative to turn our young hearts away from those we love and who love us—including God.

Pastor Jack prayed for me that God would heal that wound of rejection, and he broke the spirit of rejection off my life. Then he made an interesting observation: "Linda," he said, "I find it very ironic that your appointment with me fell on Super Bowl Sunday—the football sportsman's hallmark day of the year—one of the most important sporting events in the world! Do you realize what God is saying to you?" (I didn't!) He went on, "I believe He is saying, 'Linda, on Super Bowl Sunday, I made time for you!'"

I melted—hot tears flowed down my face. I experienced the personal, intimate heart of God probably for the first time in my life. I knew He loved me. And I knew my earthly father loved me and that my husband loved me. It was never about them rejecting me, but about their love of sports! That's not saying that their actions were always right, but I could finally let it go. I felt a freedom in my soul when I forgave and released the judgments of my heart against my dad, my husband, and God.

Let me tell you something ironic: I happen to be writing this chapter on Sunday, February 2, 2014—the date of Super Bowl XLVIII. Does God have a sense of humor or what? It certainly wasn't planned on my part. But let's continue with the story.

CHANGE AHEAD

In the following months, I began to notice that my husband was watching fewer sporting events on television. He was becoming balanced and more sensitive to my needs and the needs of our family. Amazingly I didn't say a word to change his behavior. When I released the judgment against my husband, he was released to meet my needs. My prayers were answered! It is so amazing how God works.

I once asked God, "Why do You always start the healing process with me?" His reply to my heart was, "Linda, it only requires one person in the marriage who is willing to pray and partner with Me to begin the process of healing."

Of course, we all know that it's much easier to resolve issues when both parties in a marriage are committed to participate in the process. But God can work through the prayers of just one.*

After reading my story, I wonder if you are seeing how God helped me to connect the dots to my emotions. I had experienced both anger and rejection my whole life. First I experienced them with my dad, then in other relationships not mentioned, and finally with my husband. Pastor Jack helped me to connect the dots and receive my freedom—and freedom for my family! I will always be grateful to him for his fatherly guidance. Most of all, I am grateful to my heavenly Father, who is all wisdom.

ACTIVATION EXERCISE

Get quiet before the Lord and let Him help you connect the dots between your emotions and past experiences that may be at the root of those feelings. Consider if there is a father wound (or any other wound) in your life by asking yourself the following questions. Then listen for the Holy Spirit's guidance as you consider His response.

- o Lord, will You help me identify any strong, negative emotions I exhibit in my life?

- o When did this emotion begin? When did I first feel (insert emotion: fear, intimidation, anger, rejection, hopelessness, helplessness, humiliation, shame, powerlessness, etc.)?

- o Was there a lie that I believed?

- o What is the truth?

o Lord, show me if there is anyone I need to forgive? Would You show me how You see that person?

Let the following prayer guide you in giving any father wounds (or other wounds) over to the Lord:

Father, I bring the emotion of _____ (name the emotion) to the cross today, and I ask You to cleanse my heart. Please replace that emotion with _____ (peace, forgiveness, power, confidence, innocence, hope, acceptance, etc.). Father, I forgive _____ (name the person). I release him/her and the power he/she has had over me. I also confess that I've judged _____ (name of person) for _____ (list the judgment made against the individual). Lord, I release him/her from that judgment and ask You to change him/her—and empower me to pray for him/her. I ask You to set me free in Jesus's name. Amen.

---

* It would be neglectful of me not to add that sometimes there are more intense situations where more desperate measures must be taken to bring resolution in marriages and families. We see families today struggling with bipolar disorders, addictions, extreme narcissism, and various mental diseases. I am not an expert in these areas, but I do have a little knowledge due to my years of ministry involvement. I urge you to seek professional help (preferably from a Christian counselor/psychologist/psychiatrist) when dealing with more severe cases. Sometimes God answers your prayers by leading you to someone who knows how to help you find your pathway to freedom. Pray and ask Him to lead you. Remember, whether God heals through a miracle or a process, He remains the Great Physician.

Chapter 11

BREAKING FAMILY PATTERNS

JOSIAH SOLIS IS one of the most gifted and talented young men that I know. He serves as a ministry coordinator in our Freedom department at Gateway Church and is a trained, active member of our Freedom team. He loves working with kids, and everyone in our department loves him. Although Josiah is only in his early twenties, I admire the way he has learned to manage his own soul at such a young age. That's what makes him a great Freedom guy—free people know how to free people!

Shortly after his move to Dallas in January of 2012, Josiah participated in one of my Freedom training classes on generational iniquity. Around that same time period, he attended a prophetic conference led by a minister named Kevin Weaver. During the conference, Kevin told him, "Josiah, I see that your spirit is alive and ready to change the world. However, it would be a shame if your body couldn't keep up with your spirit." For the first time, Josiah realized that he was addicted to food—fast foods especially!—and he needed to make some changes. The Freedom class and the prophetic conference became two defining moments in his life.

At the end of that generational iniquity class, I instructed the participants to ask the Lord a question: "Jesus, is there any generational iniquity that You would like to reveal to me tonight?" God spoke one word to Josiah's heart: "Obesity." It caught him off guard, but immediately God began to bring to mind various family members who were dangerously obese. Several suffered from diabetes, heart disease, and high blood pressure. In all those cases he knew the diseases were linked to obesity. When God brought that revelation to his mind, he said, "That's it!" Josiah agreed with God that Jesus had delivered him from the generational curse of obesity. The following is his story as told to me.

"I started gaining weight my senior year of high school, and that continued into my first and second years of college. A typical freshman might gain fifteen pounds," he confided to me. "Not me. I gained fifty! But I was in denial.

"People who had not seen me for six months or so would take a second glance when they saw me. I'm sure they were thinking: when did you get to be twice the size you used to be?

"I had always thought that I could manage and control my weight. I finally realized that I was lying to myself—I couldn't! My parents warned me that weight was something I must be aware of due to family tendencies toward obesity."

Josiah tried numerous fad diets to lose the weight quickly, but nothing worked.

"After we prayed that night," Josiah told me, "something felt different. I knew something had shifted." He prayed and committed to God that day, "God, You've done Your part; You've broken and healed the curse. Now it's my responsibility to eat healthy and exercise."

While he understood that he must do his part, he also knew it would be much easier now because he was no longer living under a bloodline curse. A curse is an invisible force that makes it extremely difficult or impossible to move forward because it is demonically empowered. Josiah came out of agreement with the belief systems that held the curse (consequence) intact. He stopped believing he would always struggle with his weight, that he couldn't change, and that he wasn't worthy of being at a healthy weight. He instead appropriated the blood of Christ and received the freedom that was already his for the taking the moment he asked. I'm so thankful for the Cross and the victory Jesus won!

Within six months, Josiah had lost sixty-five pounds. The first month, he lost twenty pounds with little or no effort. He changed his diet somewhat and no longer ate fast food. More than a year and a half has passed, and he has continued to keep all the weight off.

I've had Josiah share his story several times when I speak. People are always encouraged and blessed by his personal journey of freedom. After experiencing his own individual deliverance, he has a unique way of proclaiming that God cares about every detail of our life—not just whether we engage in sex, drugs, and rock and roll, but our eating habits as well. "God wanted me to be healthy," he states publicly.

Josiah's story is life-changing and a great example of unhealthy eating patterns that were linked to a family curse. Food was a drug of choice embraced by his ancestors and a weakness passed down to him, spiritually and physically.

Discovering Continuing Patterns

We have all observed families, churches, and institutions in which the same patterns are repeated over and over. Whether it is a healthy family who seems blessed beyond reason or a family that has repeated illnesses, poverty, and a history of domestic abuse and violence, we can see the same cycles of behavior generation after generation. Some churches have continual splits while others are united in purpose. Some institutions have repeated successes while others have failures or continual employee turnover. If you look closely, you will see patterns that continue over decades.

Identifying recurring patterns can be helpful as you continue your journey toward freedom. It is beneficial to determine the areas where there has been a repetitive cycle of bondage. It's not uncommon for someone to go through the process of freedom (repenting, breaking soul ties, extending forgiveness, breaking demonic oppression, etc.) yet struggle again in just a short while. When patterns of behavior in families are not dealt with at some point in the freedom process, a return to the old ways is inevitable.

Most of us still live among the people we've been around all our lives, and we're surrounded by the same behavior patterns. We often blame God when we don't get the results we'd hoped for after going through a program of deliverance and inner healing. In reality we haven't appropriated our freedom from those patterns of behavior. God did His part, but we haven't done ours. This is where counseling may need to overlap with the freedom process.

In Exodus 20 Moses talks about the sins of the fathers being visited into the third and fourth generation but the blessings of God extending to a thousand generations. God wants to bless His people, and He doesn't want us to experience curses or consequences of another's sins. Because of that, He has provided a way out! However, because those weaknesses reside in families, the enemy takes every opportunity to covertly bring destruction.

To sum it up, there are several ways blessings and curses can operate in families:

Through our spiritual heritage

Those who have gone before us in our families may have chosen to become anti-God or anti-Christ and therefore never received cleansing from their sins and from generational curses. They have passed on a spiritual heritage void of God and His ways. When we came to Christ and trusted in Him as our Lord and Savior, we became members of God's family forever. We are no longer ordinary people. We are now sons and daughters of the living God— the King of kings. We are the royalty of the universe! We have a new heritage, and we ought to live accordingly. The good news is that God has given each person on Earth a free will to choose curses or blessings!

In relationships

Parents are like a mirror we look into to give us identity. For the most part, whatever our parents told us about ourselves when we were children shapes our perceptions of who we are and our self-worth. What if they were wrong? What if they were right? For most of us they were partly right and partly wrong! As we learn to look into the mirror of our heavenly Father, we learn who we truly are. We are created in His image for greatness. And it's never too late to become who He created us to be!

Through family emotions

When we're growing up, we learn how to respond to life situations by observing those around us. If we become emotionally enmeshed with family members, where our feelings are often dictated by or dependent on others, soul ties can easily form that need to be broken. We can ask God to remove from us anything a family member or an abuser deposited in our soul. We can take back our power to choose what is right instead of what's wrong, what is healthy instead of what's unhealthy. Through forgiveness and breaking soul ties, we take back our power to live the way God intended—to live a life that produces blessings.

Bitter root judgments

Jesus tells us in Matthew 7:1 that we are not to judge. He is addressing the spirit of faultfinding that focuses on the shortcomings of others while overlooking our own. He doesn't want us to set ourselves up as the judge of others, but He isn't saying that we won't be able to recognize wrong behavior. He just means we shouldn't harden our hearts against those who do what's wrong, stop praying for them, and box them into a mold of judgment. This only serves to disable them, in our own view, from ever changing. Besides, only God is the righteous judge, and quite often He reminds me when I've become judgmental that I need to give Him back His job. It's not my business to figure out people's motives for their actions.

In the "golden oldie" movie *Gone with the Wind*, the lead character, Scarlett O'Hara, had become embittered by war, poverty, and the loss of loved ones. Thus the famous scene where she proclaims: "As God is my witness they're not going to lick me. I'm going to live through this and when it's all over, I'll never be hungry again. No, nor any of my folk. If I have to lie, steal, cheat or kill. As God is my witness, I'll never be hungry again!"[1] Scarlett positioned herself to take charge of her life (as well as the lives of her family members) when she made that famous vow. She told God what *she* was going to do. She didn't inquire of Him for help—she was too angry with Him! She set the future pattern of behavior for herself and her family, which was to pull themselves up by their own bootstraps instead of trusting and depending upon God! Do you see the generational belief system that began to brew once she made that declaration?

That's what we often do, though perhaps not so consciously or dramatically. We may never even say it out loud, but most of us have made inner vows and judgments when hard things happen to us. This causes us to develop a self-reliant attitude instead of relying on God to work things out. Jesus said we should take His yoke upon us because it is easy, and His burden is light. In Matthew 11:28–30, Jesus tells us that His "yoke" is to learn humility (our need for God) from Him. Life is never easy and our burdens are certainly never light when we take on responsibility that belongs to God. But when we learn humility from Jesus, we won't live in self-reliance—pursuing our own way. Instead, we will humbly receive His grace to help us do our part and rely upon God to do His.

When we are led by His Spirit, He empowers us to work smarter, not harder. Then we will not only enjoy His peace within our own soul, but we'll learn how to maintain peace with others. Scripture says:

> Pursue peace with all men, and the holiness without which no one will see the Lord, watching diligently so that no one falls short of the grace of God, lest any root of bitterness spring up to cause trouble, and many become defiled by it.
> —HEBREWS 12:14–15, MEV

Bitterness contaminates! When I judge someone (and refuse to extend grace), it eliminates my desire to pray for that person. Not only that, but I hurt myself in the process. Unforgiveness produces bitterness of heart, which grows like a cancer in the soul. This causes mental torment and can even lead to physical diseases. It's critical that you don't let people "own real estate in your head." Only God is qualified to be someone's judge, because only He can see what is in the person's heart. And He wants to help us see people for who they really are—their true identity. But it requires an intentional decision to see others through His eyes!

OBSERVING FAMILY HISTORY

There's nothing like a good ole family reunion to gain some insights into your family. I remember when I first began to learn about deliverance, inner healing, and life patterns. Every time I made a trip to visit my extended family, I braced for what God was about to show me. I knew He wanted to release me to new dimensions of freedom. So

I would study the nature of each family relationship and identify some corresponding events that had transpired as a result. I encourage you to consider those kinds of things the next time you are around your family. It can be very enlightening.

Most professional counselors use genograms when working with clients. These are sort of like family trees in that they are a visual representation of the family structures. But they also include facts about the members of that family to aid in analyzing hereditary or psychological factors that influence the relationships.

For example, if you're struggling with alcoholism, a genogram can help a counselor or freedom minister know if your mom or dad struggled with it too. The counselor or minister will use the genogram to observe the dynamics of families and how the members interact with one another, and then they examine the different ways those interactions affect the soul.

Seeing relational dynamics mapped out can show, for example, whether Mom has used her relationship with her son as a substitute for the one she should be having with her husband, or if Dad gets his emotional needs met through his daughter instead of his wife. Neither scenario is uncommon in families.

If you've never done a genogram, you should try it. You can find them free of charge on the web, or you can make your own. You'll be surprised how much you will learn about yourself and your family.

Whether or not you create a genogram, in order to have a thorough freedom experience you must look for:

1. Core lies we've believed

2. Soul wounds from life's events and tragedies

3. Demonic oppression

4. Life patterns that exist in families

I find it exciting to know that as I line up my will with God's will, He will lead me into my pathway of healing and freedom. He helps me to identify false belief systems that cripple me and break soul ties that create unhealthy connections to others. He gives me power over the enemy of my soul and enables me to break the life patterns handed down by my family. God has done this faithfully for me and for others. He will do it for you too as you pursue your relationship with Him.

ACTIVATION EXERCISE

Before doing the activation below, find a place with no distractions. Then quiet your heart and seek God's presence. Ask the Holy Spirit to enlighten you in the following areas:

o Lord, is there a negative pattern of behavior in my life that You want to identify?

o Did it begin with my family of origin?

o Does a family curse exist? (If so, declare that the curse has no power over your life because Jesus bore it for you, according to Galatians 3:13.)

o Are there soul ties that need to be severed? If so, sever them by praying: "Lord, I confess that I have had unhealthy connections with [name]. I realize they have controlled my actions and life in a negative way. Today, I break all unhealthy connections and break the enemy's power over my life. I ask You to be Lord over that area of my life. In Jesus's name, amen." (Some soul ties are harder to break than others, depending on how long they have been there and the depth of the tie. You must want to be completely free in order to sever some deeper ties. Feel free to pray through this prayer at a later time when you are ready to let them go.)

o What lie/lies did our family embrace? (As the Holy Spirit reveals the lies, renounce them, and come into agreement with God's Word.)

o What are some actions I can take or behaviors I can change to move toward freedom?

Here is a prayer to get you started in this activation exercise:

Father, You require me to do my part, and You will do Your part. I bring my negative behaviors to the cross. I ask You to empower me to live and walk out my freedom with victory. I renounce and break all generational bondage and ask You to replace any lies I've believed with truth. In Jesus's name, amen.

Note: Some have difficulty doing this activation alone, especially in the beginning. If you have a spiritually strong friend or mentor you trust, you might want to do this exercise with him or her. In more severe cases a professional Christian counselor may be required. God has a pathway of healing for each person. Allow Him to lead you in discovering that path.

Chapter 12

THE KENNEDY CURSE

OUNTLESS BOOKS AND articles have been written about the "Kennedy Curse." It has long been said that President Kennedy's famous family has been under a curse that has resulted in its members experiencing premature and/or unnatural deaths. While the notion of a curse can seem superstitious (and exploited for profit by an overzealous news media), it does seem more than coincidental for so many tragedies to strike one family in such a vicious and mysterious way. Let me cite some of those tragedies, in chronological order, and you can decide for yourself:

- o 1941—**Rosemary Kennedy** was believed to be mentally challenged. When Rosemary began to exhibit severe mood swings, her father, Joe Kennedy Sr., secretly arranged for her to undergo a lobotomy. It further impaired her cognitive abilities, causing Rosemary to remain institutionalized until she died in 2005.[1]

- o August 12, 1944—**Joseph P. Kennedy Jr.** died during World War II when his plane exploded while he was engaged in a dangerous mission.[2]

- May 13, 1948—**Kathleen Kennedy Cavendish**, Marchioness of Hartington (fourth child and second daughter of Joseph P. and Rose Kennedy, sister of John Fitzgerald Kennedy), died in a plane crash in France.[3]

- August 23, 1956—**Jacqueline Bouvier Kennedy** gave birth to a stillborn daughter, Arabella.[4]

- August 7, 1963—**Patrick Bouvier Kennedy** was born prematurely and died two days later.[5]

- November 22, 1963—**John F. Kennedy**, president of the United States, was assassinated in Dallas, Texas.

- June 19, 1964—US Senator **Edward M. "Ted" Kennedy** was involved in a plane crash where one of his aides and the pilot were killed. Ted Kennedy was pulled from the wreckage by a fellow senator, Birch E. Bayh, and spent months in the hospital recovering from a broken back and other injuries.[6]

- June 5, 1968—US Senator **Robert F. Kennedy** was assassinated in Los Angeles by Sirhan Bishara Sirhan immediately following his victory in the California Democratic presidential primary.[7]

- July 18, 1969—**Edward (Ted) Kennedy** accidentally drove his car off a bridge on

Chappaquiddick Island, fatally trapping his passenger, Mary Jo Kopechne, inside the vehicle. This incident caused Ted to wonder "whether some awful curse did actually hang over all the Kennedys," as he expressed in a televised statement on July 25.[8]

○ August 13, 1973—**Joseph P. Kennedy II** was the driver of a car that crashed and left a female passenger, Pam Kelley, paralyzed for life. He was convicted of reckless driving and fined one hundred dollars.[9]

○ November 17, 1973—**Ted Kennedy Jr.** had his right leg amputated because of bone cancer.[10]

○ April 25, 1984—**David Anthony Kennedy** died of an overdose of cocaine and Demerol in a hotel room in Palm Beach, Florida.[11]

○ April 1, 1991—**William Kennedy Smith** was accused of the rape of a young woman at the Kennedy estate in Palm Beach, Florida. He was later acquitted.[12]

○ December 31, 1997—**Michael LeMoyne Kennedy** died in a skiing accident in Aspen, Colorado. He was suspected of statutory rape after having started an affair with a fourteen-year-old babysitter, though he claimed the affair began when she was sixteen.[13]

○ July 16, 1999—**John F. Kennedy Jr.** died when the light aircraft he was piloting crashed into the Atlantic Ocean off the coast of Martha's Vineyard due to pilot error. His wife, Carolyn, and sister-in-law, Lauren Bessette, were also killed.[14]

- September 16, 2011—**Kara Kennedy Allen** died of a heart attack while exercising in a Washington, DC, health club. Kennedy had already suffered from lung cancer in 2002, resulting in the removal of part of her right lung.[15]

- May 16, 2012—**Mary Richardson Kennedy**, estranged wife of Robert F. Kennedy Jr., hanged herself on the grounds of her home in Bedford, New York.[16]

FAMILY PATTERNS

Regardless of your political persuasion and personal opinion of the Kennedys, the fact remains that countless members of their family have experienced premature death or were involved in tragic events. Various researchers have speculated on the origin of the Kennedy curse. Some say the curse is related to what some believe to be a biblical admonition regarding bootlegging (Isa. 5:22–23; Hab. 2:15; Prov. 20:1). Obviously these verses are subject to personal interpretation.

One source ventured to say that it originated with Joseph P. Kennedy when he secretly had doctors perform a lobotomy on his daughter, Rosemary Kennedy. It has been documented that her placid personality and erratic behavior caused her father concern. His pride and selfish ambition made him fear that she would embarrass the family and possibly damage JFK's political career. This camp supports the theory that pride is the root issue behind the curse, citing Proverbs 16:18, "Pride goes before destruction, a haughty spirit before a fall."

One reporter said Joseph Kennedy was also known to have run with gangsters, espousing racist and anti-Semitic beliefs.[17] Perhaps this is the strongest possible cause for the Kennedy curse, because the Bible tells us that anyone who curses the Jew is cursed: "I will bless them who bless you and curse him who curses you" (Gen. 12:3, MEV).

Still others believe the curse is due to the numerous adulterous affairs in which Joe Kennedy was involved. It was said that on occasion he brought his mistress, actress Gloria Swanson, home to dinner with his wife, Rose. One reporter said the Kennedys were "entitled...adulterers, whose treatment of women is historically deplorable."[18] In this case, the violation of the following commandment is a possible cause: "Thou shalt not commit adultery" (Exod. 20:14, KJV).

Joe Kennedy's sons followed in his footsteps. Bobby was unfaithful to Ethel; Ted cheated on Joan, and she plummeted into depression and alcoholism.[19] John Kennedy was a womanizer, even while in the White House. His numerous escapades allegedly caused Jackie to contemplate divorcing him during his presidency.[20] One article pointed out that until recently, JFK's relentless womanizing was contextualized as a glamorous flaw. Yet while he was serving as president, he allegedly got a teenage intern drunk and took her virginity on his wife's bed. That intern, Mimi Alford, wrote about the incident in her memoir, *Once Upon a Secret*.[21]

Most likely the Kennedys don't know exactly what force in their lives is bringing destruction and being passed from one generation to the next. Maybe they've not even considered that possibility. Perhaps they haven't come into a personal relationship with Jesus Christ. We don't know. But until someone in the family becomes aware and repents of the generational iniquity—appropriating their freedom through the blood Jesus shed for them on the cross—then the consequences of the curse will continue. God is not the force behind such tragedy—He wants to set them free. It is the evil one that comes to steal, kill, and destroy (John 10:10).

However, for every trouble the enemy brings, God has an answer. The Lord said in 2 Chronicles 7:14: "If *my* people, who are called by my name, will humble themselves and pray and seek my face and turn from their wicked ways, then I will hear from heaven, and I will forgive their sin and will heal their land" (emphasis added). And as Hosea 4:6 tells us, "My people are destroyed for lack of knowledge" (KJV).

No Curse Without a Cause

As we read earlier, "A curse without cause shall not alight" (Prov. 26:2, NKJV). That means if a curse is present, Scripture says there must be a cause. The Kennedy sin patterns we mentioned (bootlegging, pride and arrogance, selfish ambition, adultery, etc.) could be possible causes for a curse, according to the Bible.

I found the observations made by best-selling author and journalist Edward Klein to be very thought provoking. Klein was personally acquainted with many members of the Kennedy family. The premise behind his *New York Times* best seller *The Kennedy Curse* is that the Kennedy curse "is the result of the destructive collision between the Kennedys' fantasy of omnipotence—an unremitting desire to get away with things that others cannot—and the cold, hard realities of life."[22]

Please understand that we can't judge another person's heart or his motives—that is not my intent. However, Jesus did teach us that while we are not to judge one another, we can recognize the good or bad fruit produced in people's lives (Matt. 7:15–20). As for all of us, there is usually some of both. The Kennedy family simply provides an observable example for illustration purposes, but we all have stuff in our own lives and families to consider.

Having read a number of opinions and interpretations from both the Christian and non-Christian world about the so-called Kennedy curse, my personal belief is that the Kennedys believed they were above the law. The same rules did not apply to them that applied to others. The word *omnipotent*, which was used to explain Edward Klein's premise, implies having great or unlimited power. In my opinion, that suggests pride that negates the need for God. Considering that pride caused the fall of Lucifer from heaven (Ezek. 28:13–19; Isa. 14:12–15; Rev. 2:9.), it seems to be at the root of most sin in all our lives.

I don't know about you, but I am continually reminded of my personal need for God in everything I do. In fact, my life scripture is John 15:5—"For without Me you can do nothing" (MEV). I keep it on my refrigerator as a reminder of my constant need to depend upon the Lord.

For the sake of example, let's say that my opinion has some validity. What do you do if you and your family struggle with pride and self-sufficiency? What if you were raised in an environment where you believed certain rules didn't apply to you? What if you didn't feel a need for God? You may have acknowledged Jesus as Savior. You may even go to church on Sundays or attend Mass every day. Yet what would a prayer of repentance (changing your mind) look like? Let's take a minute and process that.

THE HEART MATTERS

Getting in touch with what is in our heart is not always easy, nor is it always simple to identify those areas where we are not in agreement with God. I love to reflect upon the heart because Proverbs 4:23 says out of it flow the issues (or boundaries) of life. The heart is comprised of our intellect; awareness; mind; inner person; feelings; and our deepest, innermost thoughts—our inner self. Only God knows our heart. We don't even know it sometimes until the Holy Spirit shines His light into those dark crevices of the soul that reveal our personal thoughts and intentions. In Deuteronomy 6:5, Israel is told to love the Lord "with all your heart." Jesus emphasized this priority when He was asked about the greatest commandment:

> Jesus answered him, "The first of all the command-ments is, 'Hear, O Israel, the Lord our God is one Lord. You shall love the Lord your God with all your heart, and with all your soul, and with all your mind, and with all your strength.' This is the first commandment."
>
> —MARK 12:29–30, MEV

One of the most chilling things we can do is to ask God to show us our heart. Believe me, He is faithful to show us if and when we ask. Our works may appear really good, significant, and impressive to the outside world, but God knows the motives behind our actions and is willing to show us. Sometimes what He reveals will shock the bravest of souls.

Let me give you a great personal example. Years ago I was praying for my husband—he had gotten on my last nerve about something. I was praying with real tenacity of heart, knowing God would answer my prayer by making some gigantic adjustments to his life. All of a sudden, the Holy Spirit (in a small, quiet voice) spoke to my heart: "Linda, you are not praying for Jim because you care about his soul but because *your* life will be easier if he changes." I was stunned! But it was true. I was praying from selfishness rather than compassion for Jim, and I was unable to recognize his brokenness from God's perspective.

I will admit, when my husband made some life changes later on, our entire family received the benefit of those changes—and that was a good thing. However, that should not have been the motivation behind my prayers. God wants us to care about people the way He does, and He wants to love them through us! Author Max Lucado once said, "When we love someone, we take the entire package."[23]

I want to emphasize this important truth: breaking the grip of generational iniquity is about the heart. When sin patterns are passed down from generation to generation, heart attachments to things other than God are involved. In other words, the real issue is idolatry.

BREAKING THE CURSE

Once you seek the Lord for understanding regarding your own personal sin (any attachments of the heart to wrong things) you need to determine if it is a family-of-origin issue. Ask God to open your eyes to truth and show you where you are not in agreement with Him. Find out what the Word of God has to say about the specific areas where you are struggling. Look up the scriptures on the subject and meditate on them. Let the Holy Spirit speak to your heart.

For example, let's say your greatest struggle is pride. You could look up verses such as the ones following.

> For there are six things the Lord hates—no, seven: haughtiness, lying, murdering, plotting evil, eagerness to do wrong, a false witness, sowing discord among brothers.
>
> —PROVERBS 6:16–19, TLB

Through this verse God shows us His opinion of pride.

> Pride goeth before destruction, and a haughty spirit before a fall.
>
> —PROVERBS 16:18, ASV

I believe God warns us so we can humble ourselves before experiencing a fall. In this verse God is showing us we can choose whether we are humbled before Him or before man.

> Humble yourselves in the presence of the Lord, and He will exalt you.
>
> —JAMES 4:10, NAS

This verse points out that we don't have to make things happen by pulling ourselves up by our own bootstraps! God will raise us up as we trust and depend on Him. Our part is to humble ourselves, and His part is to exalt us.

> God resists the proud [arrogant], but gives grace [help, assistance, ability] to the humble.
> —JAMES 4:6, MEV

This verse is telling us that if we need God's grace in our lives (and we all do), pride is the last thing we'd want to entertain!

If pride were the area God wanted to address in your life, after you meditated on Scripture, you'd need to ask God to show you what He wants you to know about pride. How has it affected your life? How has it touched your family? And how does He feel about what it has done? When you see things from His perspective, then you can truly experience a godly sorrow about the sin so you can connect with God's heart to pray a prayer of genuine repentance. By doing so, you come into agreement with God to break the enemy's power.

When we repent, we may not always "feel" something; in fact, often we won't experience a strong emotional reaction. Prayers of repentance aren't about feelings; they're about obedience. Some of the most dynamic, effectual prayers I've prayed did not leave me feeling deeply emotional; they were just a simple act of my will. Regardless of whether I "felt" a strong emotion at the time, those prayers were effective because they were birthed out of my relationship with my heavenly Father. The same will be true of you.

Activation Exercise

Find a place where you can be alone, quiet your heart, and listen to God's voice. Then ask God the following questions:

- Heavenly Father, what is the central area that my family (and I) struggle with?

- What lie have we believed that is in opposition to Your Word?

- What is the truth?

Below is a sample prayer you can pray to break a family curse. Remember to form your prayer in your own words according to what God has spoken to your heart. Invite the Lord's presence as you talk to Him. Here is a promise from God to give you confidence that He will show you what you need to know: "Call to Me, and I will answer you, and show you great and mighty things which you do not know" (Jer. 33:3, mev).

In the following prayer, I use pride merely as an example of how to process and connect with God in any area (ask His forgiveness, repent, and renounce and break any agreement with the enemy). Your personal struggle or issue may be something altogether different, as may the Kennedys'. Adapt this prayer as needed.

Father, Your Word tells us that every good thing given and every perfect gift is from above and comes from You (James 1:17). I ask for Your forgiveness on behalf of myself and my family for depending upon my/our own abilities to conquer, achieve, and get ahead. Forgive us for believing we are above the law and that the same rules don't apply to us as apply to others. Lord, we have sinned against You, and I ask You to cleanse my heart and the hearts of my family members. We have set ourselves up to be as God—and that is idolatry. I humble my heart before You and declare that You alone are God. There is no other God in heaven and earth, and I choose to honor and worship You!

Lord, I believe our family has lived under a curse because of the open door of pride, arrogance, and self-sufficiency. I now take my authority in Christ and break the power the enemy has had over our family. I lay the ax to the root of our family tree where pride has become a stronghold. I acknowledge our need for You.

I tell the enemy that he has no more power over our family and he must leave. I break any agreement with the enemy, and I agree with the Word of God and declare: "As I humble myself under the mighty hand of God; He will exalt me in due season" (1 Pet. 5:6). I invite the Holy Spirit to supernaturally replace pride with His humility of heart, to begin a work of restoring my heart and the hearts of my family members. Thank You, Lord, for healing our family and cleansing our bloodlines. I ask all these things in the precious name of Your Son, Jesus. Amen.

Chapter 13

WHAT IF I'M ADOPTED?

'VE SELDOM TAUGHT on generational iniquity when someone didn't come up and ask me, "What if I'm adopted? How do I deal with generational issues when I have never met my biological parents?" Needless to say, those questions would be raised in the mind of anyone who has no idea what his biological parents were like, much less the areas where they struggled.

The same principle holds true for an adopted person as for everyone else: Most of our life patterns have been established as a result of how we were raised. We are deeply influenced by the way our parents chose to live their lives—whether or not they are related to us by blood. The majority of those who were adopted never meet their biological parents, and that's perfectly fine. They can still live in freedom. When you have limited information on your blood relatives, simply deal with what you know.

For example, if you struggle with sexual issues, racism, bitterness, or control, deal with those specific issues in the same way as you would any other sin (repent, renounce, and break the tie). Using those same steps, break any unhealthy bondage or iniquity that came through the generational pipeline.

God knows the history of your biological ancestors even if you don't. Allow Him to lead you into truth by asking, "Heavenly Father, is there anything You want me to know about my family of origin? Is there a lie that I/ we have believed and embraced? What is the truth?" Then trust the Holy Spirit to lead and guide you into all truth— just as Jesus promised He would (John 16:13)—and that includes all the truth about *you*. He will reveal to you the hidden things in your past and present to better prepare you for your future!

Mark's Story

Recently I was casually greeting people in the foyer at Gateway Church as I visited with Mark Greenwood, one of our deacons. I was telling him that I was writing this book on generational iniquity. His wife, Jan, overheard our conversation and said, "Linda, you need to get Mark to tell you his story. It's something else!" Boy was she right. We set up a time to get together so I could interview him. What follows is his amazing story.

Mark's biological parents were high school sweethearts and only seventeen years old when his mother became pregnant. She kept it a secret from her parents, fearing the stigma and consequences it would bring—especially if people in their church found out. She told the birth father that she was pregnant and kept hoping he would say, "Let's get married." But for whatever reason, he never said anything. It seems he just didn't know what to do. By not making a decision, he made a decision. And Mark's birth mother was left to figure things out on her own.

Mark's young mom continued to conceal the pregnancy from her parents. She lost weight by eating nothing but Jell-O and popsicles and wearing baggy clothes. She didn't tell her mother she was pregnant until her water broke and it was time to head for the hospital!

Meanwhile in a neighboring town about seventy miles away, Mark's future adoptive parents had been trying to get pregnant. Their ob-gyn was also the doctor of Mark's biological grandmother. When Mark arrived, his biological grandmother called the doctor to inquire if he knew of a good Church of Christ family (her denomination) who would like to adopt a baby. The doctor called the couple who wanted to have a child and asked them, "Are you ready for a baby?" They had just begun discussing the possibility of adopting, so the time was right. The doctor then put the two families in touch, and Mark was adopted and taken to his new home, miles away from his birth parents.

Mark and his sister were told from the beginning that they were adopted. When Mark was only five years old, he told his adoptive mother, "Someday I'm going to find my real mother." His heart had already begun to search for them.

STRUGGLES WITH ADDICTION

Growing up, Mark struggled with addiction. He was hooked on alcohol and smoking pot by the time he was twelve years old. During his teen years, he taught Sunday school to young teens. He still remembers the lesson they were teaching: "How *not* to conform to the world." The curriculum specifically covered the dangers of doing drugs and the risks of alcohol use. During the week Mark was smoking dope daily and continued to stay stoned while selling drugs. His secret was discovered when a student pointed Mark out to a friend and remarked that he was his Sunday school teacher. His friend said, "What? He's also one of the biggest drug dealers around." The two teenagers' moms went to Mark's mom to have a conference. This resulted in Mark's dad going to the school to research the validity of the accusations. The answers weren't what he had hoped. The parents were presented pictures the school's photo club had taken using zoom lenses. The photos revealed Mark smoking pot and selling drugs.

The school suggested that Mark's dad go to the police and ask them some of the same questions. The police had already targeted three teenagers and put them in jail. The next one was to be Mark. After this Mark's dad quit his job and moved the family to another town in order to put his son in a better environment. He moved Mark from a very large 5A school to a small 1A school in a more peaceful atmosphere, hoping to involve him with a different peer group who would be a better influence.

Mark's family was highly religious. He told me in the interview, "You learn how to create a façade, which produces an atmosphere for a double life." Mark was living a performance-based life rather than developing a heart relationship with the living God.

Mark's struggle with addiction only continued. At age seventeen he passed out, drove off a cliff, and when he woke up the next morning, he determined to never touch drugs and alcohol again. He was true to his word until he was twenty-two. He went out fishing with his dad and drank some non-alcoholic beer. Mark told me it was like the inside of him lit back up again, and he actually got drunk on a non-alcoholic beverage. The addiction cycle was ignited again.

MARK STARTS HIS OWN FAMILY

Mark and his wife, Jan, met their senior year of high school, just outside of Hot Springs, Arkansas. After breaking up that summer of 1979, they went to different colleges. The following summer they started dating again, and they got married in 1983. By that time, Jan had graduated college and they moved to Abilene, where Mark attended Abilene Christian University and graduated in 1984.

Their son John was born in 1994. There were complications with the pregnancy, and mother and baby were in danger. Mark frantically cried out to the Lord in prayer. When he did, he saw Jesus sitting on the throne, and a bottle of Evan Williams whiskey was between them. Mark looked directly into Jesus's eyes. There was no condemnation there, but Mark knew the alcohol stood between them. He told Jesus that night, "I can't do this, but if You will take it, it's Yours." He never drank again.

In the past when Mark had tried to give up alcohol, it was a willpower issue. He would just turn to something else to comfort himself, like smoking or eating certain foods. This time was different. After Jesus set him free, he had no desire to drink, even if everyone around him was drinking. He needed no substitutes—Mark was free indeed!

After John was born, Mark and Jan tried everything, including fertility drugs, before they finally conceived their daughter, Ashley. When Jan was pregnant, Mark had an emotional reaction to Ashley's sonogram. He thought to himself, "Someone out there went through this with me and I've never even met her." A fire was ignited inside him to find his birth parents. All he had to go on was a name the attorney had given his adoptive mom. He tried several searches on the Internet, but they turned out to be wild goose chases. At one point he tracked down a woman he thought to be his mother, and the report revealed that she was dead. Mark was devastated. As he describes it, he crawled up in the Lord's lap and He held him all night. He stopped the pursuit to find his parents.

During that time a sales representative I'll call Craig called on Mark in his insurance business and they became friends. One day, as they were driving together on a business trip, his new friend looked at him and asked, "What's God doing in your life?" He and Mark talked for five or six hours. There had been so much happening inside of him, yet he had no one to share it with—so he just let it all out. Craig gave Mark a Christian book and became a mentor in his life. He and his wife gently walked Mark and Jan into the Spirit-filled life. Craig also gave them some books by Bible teacher Derek Prince.

They were reading *Blessing or Curse: You Can Choose* by Derek Prince when they discovered their ancestors had been involved in Freemasonry and Eastern Star. They began breaking off the Masonic curses and renounced the Freemasonry. After they broke the curses resulting from the oaths, Jan gave birth to three sons in the next few years. This was five years after Ashley was born.

BREAKTHROUGH IN THE SEARCH

After one disappointment after another in his search for his parents, Mark decided it had taken such an emotional toll on his life that he released it to the Lord. He said, "I'm done. It's Yours!" It seems that was just what God was waiting to hear. The following Monday morning he received an e-mail simply saying, "I think this is who you are looking for." It contained the full names of his biological father and mother, their dates of birth, driver's license numbers, and even their address. It was signed, "Your Adoption Angel." To this day, Mark has no idea who sent it.

It was challenging for Mark to get in touch with his birth parents due to their recent moves, but he finally was able to get a letter through to them. Then one afternoon, Mark's assistant told him he had a call from his mom. Mark and Jan went to Dallas to meet his parents at their apartment. When his dad opened the door, he and his son looked so much alike that they started laughing. As they compared notes, they discovered they both wore the same size clothes—except Mark's dad wears pants two inches shorter. They even wore the same kind of loafers, and their closets were organized just the same way.

Mark's adoptive father had worked in road construction and heavy equipment operation. Mark never had a natural aptitude for it, though he tried hard to follow in his father's footsteps. His biological father was in sales, insurance, and real estate. Those are Mark's natural abilities and what he loves. Mark had owned an insurance agency, and had purchased and remodeled homes for resale.

Mark always told Jan that his ideal retirement would be to pull an Airstream motor home throughout the country and fish. He discovered that is exactly what his biological grandfather had done before his death. In fact, his grandfather's motto was that he wanted to travel and fish until he couldn't find his way back to the campsite. Mark noted in the interview that certainly would not be Jan's idea of a great retirement. A condo in Southlake, Texas, would be just dandy for her!

During their first meeting Mark's mother asked him if he was healthy. She was very concerned for Mark's well-being because of the Jell-O and popsicles she ate to stay skinny and keep her pregnancy a secret. Also, she hadn't taken prenatal vitamins and, therefore, had always feared her baby would be sick all of his life. Fortunately Mark assured her that he was healthy and doing well.

One of Mark's first questions to his mom was, "Who in the family has struggled with alcohol?" Mark discovered that other family members had struggled with alcohol addiction as well.

Mark learned that his parents had stayed together after he was given up for adoption. Fourteen months later they had a second baby. The grandmother told them, "If you're going to keep doing this, you're getting married!" So they did.

ESTABLISHING A NEW LEGACY

Mark had always wondered why he had been so sensitive to the spiritual realm. The Holy Spirit revealed to Mark that there had been occult involvement, including divination, in his biological background. That explained why he often felt a pull toward those forbidden areas spoken of in the Bible. (See Deuteronomy 18:9–12.) The draw—or "bent"—was there early on. Fortunately he never became heavily involved.

Once the Lord revealed this iniquity to Mark, he repented for his own dabbling into those practices and on behalf of his family as well. He broke any curses (consequences) that had any legal claim in his life. Mark felt that this open door to the enemy had caused problems in his family's finances. He opened his heart to receive God's blessing (free of the enemy's hindrances) and released blessings upon his children and future generations. Mark began a new legacy that was Christ-centered.

Ever since Mark met his biological family, he has consistently connected the dots to so many areas of his life. I love the way he continues to pursue freedom in other areas of his life and claim the inheritance Christ died for him to possess.

Freedom Through Hearing God

Sometime ago, a man who had been adopted at birth came in to receive ministry. We will call him Ralph. He was addicted to pornography and had recently lost his family due to his addiction. Of course, that addiction led to other issues as well, including financial problems, relational issues, misuse of time, and difficulty establishing priorities. Ralph had been raised by wonderful, Christian adoptive parents but knew little about his biological parents.

We dealt with all the information he had been able to obtain, so now it was up to the work of the Holy Spirit. As we ministered some "listening prayer" exercises to open him up to hearing God, Ralph heard the Holy Spirit speak to his heart regarding his fourth month inside his mother's womb. He knew by the Holy Spirit that she had multiple sex partners while pregnant with him. The Holy Spirit showed him that was when the spirit of perversion entered his life. We broke that generational iniquity and its effect. And Ralph was finally free!

Keep in mind that he had already repented of his own sin and had someone to whom he held himself accountable. Ralph had done everything he knew to do—and then some! But once the spirit of perversion that gave power to the addiction was broken, he could maintain his newfound freedom. As with any addition, there is always a need for accountability with someone you trust—preferably someone trained in addictive behavior that can't be snowed!

When you've dealt with everything you know is an issue in your life, sometimes the Lord will reveal the other pieces of the puzzle. God may speak a word to you in your spirit or through a passage of Scripture, or you might uncover information through a document or by running into someone who knows your family. I've heard so many incredible stories of God giving insight to those who have been adopted. But God will do this whether or not you were adopted. He extends this invitation to all of us:

> Call to Me, and I will answer you, and show you great and mighty things which you do not know.
> —JEREMIAH 33:3, MEV

That word *mighty* in this verse means *inaccessible.* Here's another way I like to interpret that verse (this is

Linda's version, not to be confused with an official Bible translation): *Call to me, and I will answer you, and show you great and mighty things that you don't know and that you have no way of knowing unless I reveal them to you.*

I like to point out to those who are adopted that adoption is God's plan A, not plan B. As believers, we have all been adopted into God's family, and our new heritage is in Him! The following passage gives us assurance that we are the children of God.

> For you have not received the spirit of slavery again to fear. But you have received the Spirit of adoption, by whom we cry, "Abba, Father." The Spirit Himself bears witness with our spirits that we are the children of God, and if children, then heirs: heirs of God and joint-heirs with Christ, if indeed we suffer with Him, that we may also be glorified with Him.
>
> —ROMANS 8:15–17, MEV

Abba is the Aramaic word for father. We are God's children, who are dearly loved and now bear His image. As loving fathers do, He will guide us into the truth about our backgrounds, so we can experience the fullness of freedom Christ died to give.

ACTIVATION EXERCISE

If you are adopted, freedom comes in the same way as for those who know their biological parents. The only difference is the amount of knowledge you initially have to work with. Trust God to bring the pieces together for you and show you what you need to know through whatever means He chooses.

○ Ask the Lord, "Is there an iniquity in my life that You want to talk to me about?"

○ If He shows you an area of sin in your life or in your family line, ask His forgiveness and repent (agree with God's Word) for any place you have given to the iniquity. Break that agreement with the enemy.

○ Repent on behalf of your biological family and ask Jesus to cleanse your family bloodlines (to begin a new work in their lives as well as yours).

○ Make a declaration: "This iniquity stops with me!" Bring the iniquity to the cross and renounce it.

○ Now ask, "Jesus, what do You want to give me in exchange (e.g., love for hate, peace for anxiety and fear, etc.)?"

If you were adopted, let this prayer help you get started in this activation exercise:

Father, Your Word says that we have not received a spirit of slavery leading to fear again, but we have received a spirit of adoption as sons (and daughters) by which we cry out, "Abba! Father!" (Rom. 8:15, NAS). Adoption was Your idea! It wasn't Your plan B; it was Your plan A. I ask You to give me revelation knowledge related to my family of origin and my birth. I renounce the spirit of fear and the spirit of rejection that often torments those who have experienced adoption. Heal my heart and remove any emotional pain. Please give me assurance in my heart that I was wanted and planned by You—even if my biological parents didn't want me. Help me to know that I was chosen and not a mistake. In Jesus's name, amen.

If you were adopted or if you ever struggle with feelings of rejection or abandonment, remember the words of the psalmist, "Even if my father and mother abandon me, the LORD will hold me close" (Ps. 27:10, NLT).

Remember, each person is responsible for his own sin, not the sins of others. But "free people free people." As we become free, we are released to pray with power for our families and loved ones so they too may experience the freedom we have found (if they choose to receive it).

Chapter 14

CREATING A NEW LEGACY

WANT TO BEGIN this final chapter by reaffirming that your family DNA is not your destiny. You are not your father. You are not your mother. And you certainly are not your ancestors. However, the lives they led can give you valuable insight into the family patterns and habits (both good and bad) that shaped your thinking and the way you process life. Your family background contributes to how you see yourself, God, and others. Therefore, it is worth examining in the light of God's Word. Doing so will help you align your beliefs and actions with God's ways. When you do, you will be able to make lasting changes that will benefit you and your future generations.

Did you know that everyone leaves a legacy whether consciously or unconsciously? Those who are intentional about leaving a legacy will probably leave better ones. A legacy is anything handed down from one generation to another. It's not just about property and money but also about attitudes (spiritual, mental, physical, and emotional), talents, habits, and traits.

Proverbs 13:22 says: "A good man leaves an inheritance to his children's children" (MEV). The truth is that anything that you are—good or bad—will pass down to those who come after you, unless they choose differently. Having a good, godly heritage makes it much easier to choose the pathway to a blessed life.

A Fresh Start

You may be familiar with Dave Ramsey, one of America's financial gurus. Recently Dave and his daughter Rachel spoke at our church on the importance of teaching your children how to handle money. I was intrigued at their perspectives, since I was busily working on this chapter. They were, of course, speaking on leaving a financial legacy, but their talk included so much more than that.

Rachel was born at a time when her family was changing drastically. Her father, a new Christian, was learning God's way of doing things. He was also recovering from wrong choices that led to lawsuits that had taken their family into tremendous debt. To most it would seem that she was born at the worst possible time in their family history. Her siblings had enjoyed the financial "good life." But by the time she was born, they had lost everything and were deeply in debt.

Rachel's perspective of her birth is that it was at the perfect time: the time of a fresh start. The way she sees it, she didn't have to see them lose everything; instead, she got to see them rebuild their life and learn lessons that have helped countless other families get out of debt.

As I listened to Dave and his daughter, I couldn't help but be reminded of when our children were born. Jim was a new Christian, and I had just made a fresh commitment to Christ. Oh brother, did we mess up a lot! We had so much to learn—and unlearn! But it's never too late to begin a new legacy. Whether it is about money, character, integrity, relationships, faith—whatever!—God is the God of new beginnings. Sometimes it takes a while to turn the ship of our life around, but it is certainly possible on every level. The payoff is that our children will learn to follow God and think and live differently than we did. Thank God for second chances!

During one of our family's most challenging moments, the Lord spoke encouraging words to me one morning in my quiet time. He said, "Don't be discouraged, for out of your lineage will come many great men and women of God." It was so crystal clear that it was almost audible, and I immediately recorded it in my journal. At the time, it didn't seem possible—even now it is a stretch to believe all the things He told me. But God never lies, and He is faithful to keep His promises.

One morning as I was rocking my baby granddaughter, London, the Lord spoke to me and said, "She has your heart." I smiled because London just loves me! Ever since she was a toddler, she has asked me questions about Jesus. With each of my grandchildren, I would pray and proclaim God's destiny over them as I rocked them to sleep. I'm not exactly sure how God's word to me will come to pass, because He didn't give me specifics, but I know it will.

To the best of my ability, I've poured my life into my family. I've failed many times to do it perfectly (in fact, "forgive me" is my middle name), but I've done my best. God willing, there will be more opportunities to pour what Jesus has given me into my children and grandchildren. I hunger for them to know the importance of practicing the presence of God and hearing His voice. I desire that they know their authority in Christ as they feed upon

His Word. I want them to learn to forgive quickly and not allow offenses to accumulate. May they be aware of the importance of every word they speak about themselves and others! And, most of all, may they be aware of what is in their hearts—where their affections lie. I pray that God will be number one in their hearts.

Books written on leaving a legacy always ask questions such as, "What would you like your epitaph to say?" or, "How do you want to be remembered?" I'm not sure just yet. I have a few years to figure it out—at least I think I do. But I do know one thing: I want to influence my children, grandchildren, and (I hope) great-grandchildren to love God and trust Him with their lives. I want them to make a difference in the world—to leave godly footprints.

Godly or Ungodly Heritage

All Christian parents should have the goal of leaving a godly legacy. Parents are God's representatives on earth to influence their children through their prayers, words, and example. Then they must trust the Holy Spirit to work in the hearts of their sons and daughters.

Jonathan and Sarah Edwards were great examples of leaving a godly heritage for their eleven children. He was a Puritan preacher who lived in the 1700s. Derek Prince also used this example in his book *Blessing or Curse: You Can Choose* to illustrate what a difference it can make to raise your children according to God's Word:

A man named A. E. Winship decided to trace the descendants of Jonathan Edwards one hundred and fifty years after he died. He found an incredible legacy from the Edwards family and contrasted it to that of a man named

Max Jukes. Jukes's legacy was tracked through forty-two men in the New York prison system. Take a look at the lives of these two men and their descendants, and no one will ever convince you that one generation doesn't influence another!

Jonathan Edwards's godly legacy produced:

- One US vice president
- Three US senators
- Three governors
- Three mayors
- Thirteen college presidents
- Thirty judges
- Sixty-five college professors
- Eighty public office holders
- One hundred lawyers
- One hundred missionaries[1]

Max Jukes's descendants included:

- Seven murderers
- Sixty thieves
- Fifty women of debauchery
- One hundred thirty other convicts
- Three hundred ten professional paupers (with over 2,300 years lived in poorhouses)

- o Four hundred decendants who were physically wrecked by indulgent living[2]

- o It was estimated that Max Jukes's descendants cost the state more than $1,250,000.[3]

This is such a powerful contrast showing how much a parent's influence and leadership can affect his children. For many of you, it has been up to you to begin a new family legacy, to change the direction of your family from an ungodly heritage to a godly one. Or perhaps you were responsible for turning the tide of family dynamics by instilling godly character and integrity. I've met many families who are first-generation believers in Jesus and have successfully fought the good fight in steering their families toward a godly heritage. With God's help, we all have the power to change the course of our families and begin a new legacy for generations to come. Let it be said of me when my life is over: "I have fought a good fight, I have finished my course, and I have kept the faith" (2 Tim. 4:7, MEV).

TAKING BACK WHAT THE ENEMY STOLE

No doubt, your family influenced who you are today. None of our parents were perfect, and you won't be either. It's almost unbelievable that something as small as an inner vow spoken in a time of anger can set in motion an attitude that will affect generations to come. I'm so thankful that we parents get "do-overs" to impact those in our family tree more positively.

Now please do not misunderstand me. I am not saying you and your ancestors are totally responsible for the behavior or moral character of your children. God *does* hold you accountable for training your children in His ways, but He will hold *them* accountable for whether or not they heed your training and follow Him. If your child or teen behaves badly or walks away from God, he cannot write it off by saying, "My gene pool made me do it." There are plenty of kids who have ungodly parents and absolutely no one in their family tree who has ever known the Lord, yet that child or teen chooses to receive Jesus as their Savior.

On the other hand, there are many godly parents who have set a wonderful example for their children, yet they may have a child who rebels against God and everything his parents tried to teach him. We all have been given the free will to decide whether or not we will give in to peer pressure, selfishness, and the ways of the world, and that decision can occur with or without generational iniquity at work.

The thing to remember is that there is great power in a parent's prayers. God is always gracious to rescue those who will call upon Him, and He knows how to deliver anyone from the enemy's grip. You have the power in Jesus's name to take back the ground given over to the enemy (2 Cor. 10:3–4). The next generation has the potential of being better prepared so they don't have to deal with the same bondages you did. Once strongholds of wrong thinking have been demolished in your life, you and your family will be ready to take back what the enemy has stolen. As you begin living in obedience to God, He will restore what has been lost.

IMPARTING A BLESSING

I recently taught a training class for pastors and leaders on the importance of several things our mothers typically impart to us, such as nurturing and comfort. Beforehand, one of our freedom pastors, Tommy Briggs, taught on father wounds, and he emphasized the significance of a father's impartation of blessing to his sons and daughters.

In my session I began by describing several mothering styles. Then I asked forgiveness on behalf of mothers who had wounded their sons and daughters—most often without intention (what I did is called representational repentance). Finally I spoke a mother's blessing over the adults who were present. When I looked out across the audience, I was shocked to see men and women wiping away tears. A few sobs could be heard. My heart was deeply touched, to say the least.

Afterward several people asked for copies of the mother's blessing that I spoke over them. Evidently it had deeply impacted their lives; and since they were leaders, I feel sure they wanted to share it with others. I only mention this to make a point. Many people never had their mother *or* father bless them. We all need that so much! God created us with that need, and there is a void in our heart if we don't receive our parents' blessing.

Never cease to bless your children every chance you get. The blessing of a father and mother is not a one-time thing but a lifetime process of encouragement. It should reflect the kind of reassurance we receive from our heavenly Father—never condemning or critical but positive, encouraging, and loving. Whenever we fall down, He always picks us up. When we are weak, He strengthens us. We should aspire to give that kind of love to our children, because it will be a powerful influence to point them to God.

I urge you to chart the course of freedom for your children—and run it yourself. Show them the way! Remember that the choices you make today will impact both you and your family. God has promised those who love Him that He will bless our children to a thousand generations. You can break the chains forged by past generations, experience freedom in your life today, and leave a lasting legacy.

ACTIVATION EXERCISE

As always, find a place where you can be alone, quiet your heart, and listen to God's voice. Then consider the following questions:

- How do you want your epitaph to read?

- What legacy do you want to leave your children and grandchildren?

- Ask the Lord, "Father, in what ways can I bless my children and grandchildren to ensure I leave a godly legacy?"

Let this prayer get you started as you consider the legacy God would have you leave:

> *Father, the desire of my heart is to leave a lasting, godly legacy for my family. Lead me by Your Spirit so my life will reflect Your heart in*

everything I do and say. I ask that Your hand be powerfully upon my family and future descendants. Allow us to be recipients of the grace and blessing that are transmitted from You to all future generations and the world. In Jesus's name, amen.

CONCLUSION

T HIS BOOK WOULDN'T be complete without addressing the subject of aftercare—that is, maintaining your freedom. You have learned in these fourteen chapters the importance of understanding your family of origin and getting free of any generational patterns that may be binding and hindering your life. Whether the Lord has shown you the importance of freedom from family financial bondage, paralyzing fear, or father or mother wounds, it is important to stay free once you have tasted liberty. Galatians 5:1 says, "For freedom Christ has set us free; stand firm therefore, and do not submit again to a yoke of slavery" (ESV).

When we are truly free, we have the ability to move without constraint through life and our spheres of influence. Freedom is not just about doing what we want to do and enjoying the good life, though I hope we all will experience some of that too! True freedom gives us the ability to connect with God without hindrance and to those individuals with whom we enjoy relationship—those we love and care for. That is worth fighting for in my book, and worth learning to live and maintain our freedom.

Much of aftercare is maintaining our connection to God, or practicing His presence. Scripture tells us that "where the Spirit of the Lord is, there is freedom" (2 Cor. 3:17, ESV). When I share that with people, the next question is always, "How do I practice God's presence?" While I'm hesitant to give a to-do list, there are some basic things we as followers of Christ should be mindful of in order to stay free.

Stay alert

The enemy will try to regain the territory he's lost. When Satan tempted Jesus in the wilderness, he left for a season, but Scripture says he waited for a more opportune time to return (Luke 4:13). We must be wise and ask the Lord for a discerning heart to know when the enemy is crouching at our door and be alert to his lies. Submit to God; resist the devil, and he will flee.

Maintain consistent, honest communication with God

Commit to meet with Him every day in prayer and fellowship. When I begin my day with prayer, I am prepared to face whatever comes my way. It is amazing the difference it makes.

Read the Bible daily

Meditate on God's Word. The Bible tells us the truth sets us free (John 8:32) and that God's Word is truth (John 17:17). Only by knowing the truth can we truly walk in freedom.

Keep in community

Attend church and build relationships with other believers. If you find yourself returning to old patterns of thinking, actions, and feelings, talk with a trusted friend or counselor who will pray for you and encourage you. We need one another. God made us to be interdependent—not dependent or independent.

Consistently take negative or false thoughts captive

Reject lies the enemy feeds you. Stand in truth. Keep fighting to maintain your freedom in Christ.

Remember, there are times when God may be leading you into a deeper level of healing. It's been said that living in freedom is like peeling an onion—there are many layers to be addressed. We often need healing in the same area at a deeper level. I have often said, "But Lord, we've already worked on that!" or, "I've already been freed in that area of my life." More often than not, there are deeper levels for me to contend with. Sometimes we have received a level of freedom, and we believe and confess the truth, but our hearts may be rooted in old negative thinking that doesn't want to lose its ground. We must be vigilant to deal with these issues as often as necessary so we can experience all God has for us.

Walking in freedom is a continual process—it never ends. But it is worth the effort. And remember, the Lord wants you to be free. The psalmist said, "In my distress I prayed to the Lord, and the Lord answered me *and set me free*" (Ps. 118:5, NLT, emphasis added).

NOTES

CHAPTER 1
YOUR ORIGINS MATTER

1. Beth Moore, *Breaking Free* (Nashville, TN: B&H Publishing Group, 2007), 107.
2. John and Paula Sandford, *Healing the Wounded Spirit* (Tulsa, OK: Victory House Publishers, 1985).

CHAPTER 2
CHARTING THE COURSE

1. Caroline Leaf, *Switch On Your Brain* (Grand Rapids, MI: Baker Books, 2013).
2. BibleHub.com, Strong's Hebrew #5771, *avon*, accessed November 6, 2015, http://biblehub.com/hebrew/5771.htm.

CHAPTER 3
BIBLICAL PATTERNS OF GENERATIONAL INIQUITY

1. Edward Mote, "My Hope Is Built on Nothing Less," 1837. Public domain.

CHAPTER 4
EMPOWERED TO SUCCEED

1. Dr. James B. Richards, *Wired for Success: Programmed for Failure* (Travelers Rest, SC: True Potential, Inc., 2010).
2. Oswald Chambers, quoted in R. G. Wolins, *Everyday Optimum Leadership: Practicing Servant Leadership* (Nashville, TN: WestBowPress, 2012), 152.

CHAPTER 7
SPIRITUAL GENETICS TRANSFER

1. Dr. Caroline Leaf, *Who Switched Off My Brain?* (Nashville, TN: Thomas Nelson, 2009), 38.

CHAPTER 9
TYPE O + TYPE O = TYPE O—SO WHY AM I TYPE A?

1.   Earl G. Graves, quoted in Nathaniel M. Lambert, *Publish and Prosper: A Strategy Guide for Students and Researchers* (New York: Routledge, 2014), 85.

CHAPTER 11
BREAKING FAMILY PATTERNS

1.   *Gone with the Wind*, directed by Victor Fleming (Beverly Hills, CA: Metro-Goldwyn-Mayer, 1939).

CHAPTER 12
THE KENNEDY CURSE

1.   Eleanor Goldberg, "JFK's Sister's Lobotomy Was 'Tragic Choice,' New Book About Disabilities Reveals," *Huffington Post Online*, November 12, 2014, accessed August 10, 2015, http://www.huffingtonpost.com/2014/11/12/tim-shriver-fully-alive_n_6141734.html.

2.   "Early John F. Kennedy Letter about the Death of His Brother Joe—The Event Which Would Propel Him into Politics," Shapell, accessed September 8, 2015, http://www.shapell.org/manuscript/jfk-kennedy-family-joe-death. See also "Joseph Patrick Kennedy," *Military Times*, accessed September 8, 2015, http://valor.militarytimes.com/recipient.php?recipientid=21302.

3.   "Kathleen Kennedy," John F. Kennedy Presidential Library and Museum, accessed September 8, 2015, http://www.jfklibrary.org/JFK/The-Kennedy-Family/Kathleen-Kennedy.aspx.

4.   Carl Anthony, "The Children of Jacqueline Kennedy," FirstLadies.org, September 19, 2013, accessed August 10, 2015, http://www.firstladies.org/blog/the-children-of-jacqueline-kennedy/.

5.   Steven Levingston, "For John and Jackie Kennedy, the Death of a Son May Have Brought Them Closer," *Washington Post*, October 24, 2013, accessed August 10, 2015, https://www.washingtonpost.com/opinions/for-john-and-jackie-kennedy-the-death-of-a-son-may-have-brought-them-closer/2013/10/24/2506051e-369b-11e3-ae46-e4248e75c8ea_story.html.

6. Ned Potter, "Edward M. Kennedy Escaped Death in 1964," ABC News, August 27, 2009, accessed August 10, 2015, http://abc news.go.com/Technology/story?id=8271369.

7. "This Day in History, June 5, 1968: Bobby Kennedy Is Assassinated," History.com, accessed August 10, 2015, http://www .history.com/this-day-in-history/bobby-kennedy-is-assassinated.

8. "This Day in History, July 18, 1969: Incident on Chappaquid-dick Island," History.com, accessed August 10, 2015, http://www .history.com/this-day-in-history/incident-on-chappaquiddick -island. See also "Primary Resources: Ted Kennedy's Post-Chappa quidick Speech," *American Experience*, accessed August 10, 2015, http://www.pbs.org/wgbh/americanexperience/features/primary -resources/kennedys-post-chappaquidick/.

9. Peter S. Canellos, *Last Lion: The Fall and Rise of Ted Kennedy* (New York: Simon & Schuster, 2009).

10. Tribune Wire Services, "Ted's Son Has Cancer; Leg Will be Amputated," *Chicago Tribune*, November 17, 1973, http:// archives.chicagotribune.com/1973/11/17/page/33/article/surgery -set-for-today.

11. United Press International, "Kennedy Probe Reveals Dismal Days: Friends Say David Was Depressed, Talked of Drug Habit Before His Death," *Orlando Sentinel*, June 9, 1985, accessed August 10, 2015, http://articles.orlandosentinel.com/1985-06-09 /news/0300370127_1_drug-overdose-kennedy-palm-beach.

12. Associated Press, "Key Events in Case," December 12, 1991, *Los Angeles Times*, December 12, 1991, accessed August 10, 2015, http://articles.latimes.com/1991-12-12/news/mn-317_1_william -kennedy-smith-case.

13. "The 'Kennedy Curse,'" *San Antonio Express-News*, accessed August 10, 2015, http://www.mysanantonio.com/news /slideshow/The-Kennedy-Curse-74297/photo-5480204.php.

14. Liz McNeil, "John F. Kennedy Jr. and Carolyn Bessette: The Way They Were," *People*, August 6, 2014, accessed August 10, 2015, http://www.people.com/article/john-f-kennedy-jr-carolyn -bessette-kennedy-fifteen-year-after-deaths.

15. Susan Donaldson James, "Kara Kennedy's Heart May Have Taken 'Direct Hit' by Cancer Cure," ABC News, September 20, 2011, accessed August 10, 2015, http://abcnews.go.com/Health /kara-kennedys-heart-attack-related-cancer-treatment/story ?id=14558232.

16.   Christina Ng and Richard Esposito, "Robert F. Kennedy Jr.'s Estranged Wife, Mary Richardson Kennedy, Dead in Apparent Suicide," *Good Morning America*, May 16, 2012, accessed August 10, 2015, http://abcnews.go.com/US/robert-kennedy-jrs-estranged-wife-mary-richardson-kennedy/story?id=16362607.

17.   Maureen Callahan, "The Real Curse of the Kennedys," *New York Post*, May 20, 2012, accessed August 10, 2015, http://nypost.com/2012/05/20/the-real-curse-of-the-kennedys/.

18.   Ibid.

19.   Laura Lippman, "Two Books Unveil Details, From Sex to Silverware," *Baltimore Sun*, August 12, 1994, accessed August 25, 2015, http://articles.baltimoresun.com/1994-08-12/features/1994224029_1_ethel-kennedy-bobby-kennedy-kennedy-women; Stanton Peele, "The Top Seven Kennedy Sex Scandals," *Psychology Today*, May 21, 2008, accessed August 25, 2015, https://www.psychologytoday.com/blog/addiction-in-society/200805/the-top-seven-kennedy-sex-scandals.

20.   Bill Hutchinson, "Explosive New Biography Reveals Jackie Kennedy Was Set to Divorce JFK Before Assassination," *New York Daily News*, June 3, 2014, accessed August 25, 2015, http://www.nydailynews.com/entertainment/gossip/explosive-biography-jackie-kennedy-set-divorce-jfk-article-1.1815810.

21.   Callahan, "The Real Curse of the Kennedys."

22.   Edward Klein, *The Kennedy Curse: Why Tragedy Has Haunted America's First Family for 150 Years* (New York: St. Martin's Press, 2003), back cover.

23.   Max Lucado, *A Love Worth Giving: Living in the Overflow of God's Love* (Nashville, TN: Thomas Nelson, 2002), 193.

CHAPTER 14
CREATING A NEW LEGACY

1.   A. E. Winship, *Jukes-Edwards: A Study in Education and Heredity* (Harrisburg, PA: R. L. Myers & Co., 1900), accessed August 11, 2015, http://www.gutenberg.org/files/15623/15623-h/15623-h.htm.

2.   Ibid.

3.   Ibid.

ABOUT THE AUTHOR

Linda Godsey serves as one of the freedom pastors at Gateway Church in Dallas/Fort Worth, Texas. Whether through writing, speaking, training, or personal ministry, she has a passion to share the message of freedom and to see people set free and experiencing their destiny in Christ. A regular speaker at Gateway's quarterly KAIROS freedom event, she also helps train churches nationally and internationally that desire to establish a freedom ministry.

Linda has been in ministry for over thirty years, serving in freedom, women's, and small-group ministry. She has been a conference and retreat speaker, and has written numerous devotionals for various Christian websites and magazines. Her first book, *Letting Go: Seeing Regret from God's Perspective*, was published in 2013.

She and her late husband, Jim, spent sixteen years at The Church on the Way in Van Nuys, California, where they were trained in ministry under the pastorate of Jack Hayford. The couple served as elders and in several other ministries, including Cleansing Stream, a freedom and inner healing ministry. During her time at The Church on the Way, Linda also completed the School of the Bible founded by Dr. Hayford.

Linda has two loving daughters and sons-in-law, two precious granddaughters, and four amazing grandsons.